Have it your way

Have it your way

52 brilliant ideas for getting everything you want

Nicholas Bate

brilliantideas

CAREFUL NOW

Arm yourself with the ideas in this book and you should find you get your way in all kinds of situations. But don't expect to get it right straight away – these are skills you have to work at – if at first you don't suceed ... you'll get there in the end. Just remember to use your new powers wisely, and don't be tempted to turn to the dark side.

Copyright © The Infinite Ideas Company Limited, 2008

The right of Nicholas Bate to be identified as the author of this book has been asserted in accordance with the Copyright, Designs and Patents Act 1988.

First published in 2008 by
The Infinite Ideas Company Limited
36 St Giles
Oxford, OX1 3LD
United Kingdom
www.infideas.com

A CIP catalogue record for this book is available from the British Library

ISBN 978-1-905940-46-2

Brand and product names are trademarks or registered trademarks of their respective owners.

Designed and typeset by Baseline Arts Ltd, Oxford
Cover designed by Cylinder
Printed in India

Brilliant ideas

Brilliant features

Each chapter of this book is designed to provide you with an inspirational idea that you can read quickly and put into practice straight away.

Throughout you'll find three features that will help you get right to the heart of the idea:

- *Here's an idea for you* Take it on board and give it a go – right here, right now. Get an idea of how well you're doing so far.

- *Defining idea* Words of wisdom from masters and mistresses of the art, plus some interesting hangers-on.

- *How did it go?* If at first you do succeed, try to hide your amazement. If, on the other hand, you don't, then this is where you'll find a Q and A that highlights common problems and how to get over them.

Introduction

Who do you want to influence? Your boyfriend about his smoking? Your mum to reduce her very long and tiring commute? The council about their lack of support for bicycles in the city? Everybody wants to influence somebody.

Much of life is actually about influencing – the ebb and flow of conversations and relationships; of long-term wishes versus short-term desires; of the pragmatic versus the visionary; of his versus hers. Influencing is a great skill to have and the ideas in this book will help you become brilliant at it.

This book is definitely for you if you want to:

- Improve a relationship
- Increase your salary
- Sort out a dispute with the neighbours
- Get a better deal from the bank
- Get help from someone
- Get a refund
- Improve your campaigning strength
- Stop your toddler's dreadful public behaviour
- Change the world

It's a book for you if you want to change someone, or something.

Because it permeates so much of everyday life, influencing is a tremendous skill for you to sharpen. It's very rare that we and another person totally agree with each other. Sometimes it doesn't matter; but sometimes it's a serious problem, so we need to influence them. And that's when the challenge begins! It's a rare person who will 100% agree with us fundamentally; it's a rare person who will change their mind simply and quickly just to accommodate us.

You don't like my messiness in the flat? Fine, I can re-invent myself. You don't like the lack of support for bicycles? No problem, we can invest one million euros in new cycleways. You don't like our overdraft charges? Okay, we can drop them for you. Not very likely is it?

So, how does change happen? How do we influence? How do you get it your way? How do you avoid the arguments and rows, the suffocating frustration, the long sulks, the door slamming and nasty e-mails?

All good influencing is a mixture – in varying proportions depending on the circumstances – of logic and emotion. Logic is the flow of the argument to influence: the facts, the circumstances, the backgrounds and exactly what is wanted. Emotion is about person-to-person connection. It entails listening, sensitivity, reasonableness and flexibility. Put the two (logic and emotion) together and you get a heady cocktail. This book will ensure you use them brilliantly. You'll then be prepared to deal with any situation:

- Your daughter's physics teacher who seems to have written her off as having no science ability.
- The hardware shop that sold you a 'dud' barbecue and seems unwilling to do anything about it.
- The insurance company who didn't clarify a major drawback to the policy.
- Your desire to break the ice and start talking again to your cousin from Sydney.

Of course, the reality is that many of the challenges in life start, at their core, with an influencing need.

You want to lose weight: it's not really about a diet, it's about influencing your mum to accept that you are going to eat smaller meals – and, when you do, you won't 'waste away'.

You want a career change: it's not about a better CV, it's about influencing your current employer into realising that you have more potential than a page of CV will reveal.

You want to reduce stress: it's not about learning meditation, it's about influencing your two teenagers to help more around the house.

Yes, influencing is everything. This book will ensure you are brilliant at having it your way!

And where do the ideas come from that are in this book? I've been very fortunate in my career to date (firstly in a variety of organisations and now running a consultancy) to work with a whole range of people in hundreds if not thousands of different situations. I've seen what works and what definitely doesn't work. Also, given that much of my life is spent teaching and consulting, I've seen what helps people understand these ideas as quickly as possible. The ideas are simple, but not simplistic. Quick to learn, but long-lasting in effect. Easy, but not silly. For home and for work. For your husband and for the kids. For your boss; for the builders; for the vicar. They'll influence anybody to anything. And it's all in this book

What about you? You just need to read an idea and try it. You'll love your improved ability to work with people and get things done that the ideas in this book give to you.

Am I bold enough to say you'll always be able to have it your way? Not quite, but I am confident that you will become very good, very quickly at having it your way a lot of the time and the rest of the time making huge progress towards that goal. So, go on: it's time to start becoming brilliant at influencing and *have it your way.*

1

How to read minds

To have it your way, you need to know what the other person is thinking and how they are currently feeling. Then you'll know how they'll respond to you.

Being a mind reader is about relating to others' concerns and understanding why they are resisting. It's time to 'get into their shoes' and understand 'where they are coming from'.

One of the best and fastest ways to influence someone is to be able to understand the way the other person ticks – what they think and feel. We know what's on our own minds, of course: the boyfriend who never tidies up after himself; the teenage daughter coming home well after curfew (and not even apologising); or the bank manager who seems to have changed his mind after agreeing to that cheap business loan.

But what was on *their* minds when they made those 'decisions'? The boyfriend *must* know it annoys us when he drops his towel on the floor, surely? The daughter *must* know we are worried when she is home late, surely? The bank manager *must* know this could harm our business growth, surely?

Here's an idea for you...

Sit quietly somewhere. Close your eyes and clear your mind. Now imagine in your mind's eye the person you wish to influence; imagine them talking to you. Then imagine what they are thinking – no, not what *you* are thinking, what *they* are thinking. Imagine what they are feeling. Imagine what they are saying. Notice how your perspective suddenly shifted. Notice how you felt a lot more perceptive and open to their perspective and got some good ideas on how to approach the problem. With practice, you'll soon get really good at this.

Sadly, they probably don't! Most people don't think very much about the other person's perspective – but it doesn't matter because you do and you're going to be brilliant at it.

Here's what to do. Stop thinking about you for a moment – you know that part! Think about them, the person you want to influence. Imagine you are a detective in a police show. Imagine posing questions such as: why would it be sensible for them to do that apparently odd behaviour?

More importantly, imagine the answers: 'I drop the towels because they magically get picked up' ... 'I come home late because my friends think I'm cool because I can do that' ... 'I changed my mind about the loan because you didn't get back to me promptly so I didn't think you were that interested'.

Then ask: if I were them, what would get me to change?

- 'If I realise that the dropped towels are no longer magically getting picked up and they would soon start to stink.'

- 'If I could look cool in other ways.'

- 'If I had a carefully worded e-mail.'

See – it's a great approach to finding leverage for what you want. Granted, like most things, it may need a bit of practice but it's worth the effort. You'll be amazed at how quickly you can begin to 'see' the other point of view, and how quickly you can realise how one 'crazy' perspective can seem perfectly sane to another person.

Plus, of course, it'll help you to be seen as a person who respects the view of others, which will make it even easier to *have it your way*.

'We can never judge the lives of others, because each person knows only their own pain and renunciation. It's one thing to feel that you are on the right path, but it's another to think that yours is the only path.'
PAULO COELHO, author

Defining idea

'Before you judge a man, walk a mile in his shoes. After that, who cares? He's a mile away and you've got his shoes.'
BILLY CONNOLLY, comic and actor

Defining idea...

3

How did it go?

Q Why should I try to understand the way they are thinking and what they are feeling? After all, they are wrong and I need this behaviour to stop.

A *You are probably right: they probably are wrong. But it's worth remembering that when we influence, it is not just what we say, but the way that we say it. Once we realise that our teenage daughter feels we are treating her as if she were a toddler, we can explain things in a different way. 'Reading her mind' is a means to an end. When we attempt to 'read their mind', it is certainly not a sign of weakness on our part – it's simply ensuring that we are doing our utmost to increase our chances of avoiding deadlock argument and ensuring you 'have it your way' as quickly as possible. Plus it's fun!*

Q This is a bit 'touchy-feely' for me. How's it going to help if I just need my sales people to work harder?

A *Okay, you want them to work harder for you. The question is, how? A really good starting point is to understand 'where they are coming from'. And if they currently feel that the new compensation scheme is a stitch-up, we're off to a bad start. If we listen, understand and respond, we have a chance to win them over. And of course, if we successfully win them over, they are much more likely to work harder. The funny thing about motivating someone to ensure you have it your way is that it's less about controlling or shouting but more about understanding and listening. It is simple, really.*

2

What must you get? And what would be nice?

Of course you want the other person to change. Of course you want other things too. But, what changes do you insist on and what things would just be 'nice'?

Surprisingly, a good way to have it your way is to be more flexible and consider the options a little more. More options: more flexibility. More flexibility: better chance of having it your way.

When we are influencing somebody – perhaps to encourage them to let us borrow their amazing SLR digital camera for our trip to South America or to get them to stop playing loud music on a Sunday morning – we of course know what we *want*: the camera; the silence; the camera in our bag; the music off. But what happens if that's not possible? We can't have it all, can we? Our friend says the camera is simply in too much use to lend out; the music is being played by a shift worker and that's the only time she can listen to her CDs.

Here's an idea for you...

To help you explore the options easily, write them down on a bit of paper. Draw three columns. Use column 1 to list broadly what things you want: the plumber's bill reduced; the camera loan; time off work that means you can comfortably travel to your friend's wedding venue. Alongside these wants, write down the ideal outcomes in column 2: the plumber doesn't charge anything for his follow-up visit to solve the problem properly; your mate's top-of-the-range SLR camera; the boss gives you the whole Friday off. Then, in column 3, what *must* you get? A refund on the labour if not the parts; any camera that will take decent photos; the boss's OK to leave at lunchtime.

Will we be unable to get what we want? Have we lost? Of course not – we're not giving up that easily – because we have already given some thought to what we *must* have and what is *just nice*. What we must have is a decent digital camera for our trip; it doesn't *have* to be that specific camera. What we *must* get is some catch-up sleep at the weekend; it doesn't *have* to mean that our neighbour turns off her music. We're keeping an eye on the bigger picture.

On a practical note, take a moment to think before you act. There's some influencing you need to do. What's *really* important about this discussion you're going to have? And what's *quite* important? You want your mate's digital camera for your Andean trip because it's the best. That's what you really want. But, think again. What you actually need, of course, is just any decent camera. So, maybe if he won't lend you his, he will know someone else you could ask. Or maybe, as he's a bit of a camera buff, he's got another one you can borrow.

What about this early morning music on Sundays? You want her to shut up. But she's a nurse, working gruelling shift patterns, and listening to music is her way to relax. You don't really begrudge her that, do you? So, maybe what we want here is to get a friendship going, so that then we can talk to her about your need for sleep. Of course, it is going to take a little longer but it is likely to work and any arrangement you make will stick. It's certainly better than falling out with a neighbour.

Makes sense, doesn't it? What we're doing is asking, what would be nice, but what must we get? This doesn't mean we are losing out on what we originally wanted – we're simply being flexible; we're considering the bigger picture, the longer term and above all the relationship. And all of these are, of course, equally valuable.

It is rarely a one-off battle to *have it your way*. You'll need to be discussing further issues with your boss, the council or with your mum. Hence, all of us need to take a regular reality check on what we are seeking.

Defining idea...

'*Negotiation in the classic sense assumes parties more anxious to agree rather than to disagree.*'
DEAN ACHESON, US lawyer and statesman

Q   Wouldn't I be better just sticking to what I want?

A   *Perhaps, but bear in mind that this is not at all about giving up. It's just that sometimes we get so fixed on getting exactly what we want that it can actually block us getting anything at all. For example, you want a pay rise but perhaps some company contribution to your train season ticket will do just as well. Keep thinking 'nice to have' and 'must have'. Of course the best SLR camera has sparked our desire and possibly even inspired us, but it is not essential – what we need is a camera. When influencing, it is vital to have a mindset and approach that is 'I want this to be something – as far as possible – which is good for both of us'. Never approach it as an exercise in 'winning'. If you do, you are likely to alienate the other person or get an agreement that won't stick.*

Q   But what about the cases where there's no difference between 'must have' and 'nice to have'?

A   *It may seem that way at first, but when you think about it a bit and when you give it time, there always is a bit of a range from 'nice to have' to 'must have'. Say you need to influence your landlord to fix the leaking roof. It seems as if there is only one option: 'must have' the roof fixed now. But in fact 'nice to' is fix the roof today, whereas 'must have' is an agreement to fix the roof at the landlord's convenience but with some rent rebate for damage and inconvenience.*

3
Become a people wizard

People are so, so different. Understanding that fact helps you to become a wizard at reading them. That's important when working to have it your way.

Unless you're one of truly identical twins, everybody in the world will approach a challenging situation differently to you. To influence them you need to tap into their way of working.

An easy way to get into a mess when influencing is to assume people will see 'our logic'. Of course, you see it as logical to start saving now so you can get on the property ladder. Unfortunately, your boyfriend sees it as logical to splash out and enjoy life now.

People see things differently. It's odd that answers we think will be common to all of us – i.e. an 'obvious' or 'right' way to approach a problem or a 'logical' way to sort it out – don't really exist. You've probably noticed this when, perhaps, discussing a film with a friend: you were insistent that the hero shouldn't have done something but your buddy has disagreed. How on earth did they see it that way?

Here's an idea for you... Take a sheet of paper and jot down the names of some people you find it very hard to influence: your dad or that builder who is brilliant at his job but will never budge on prices. Against each name, write down what annoys you so much about them – e.g. their stubbornness, procrastination …. Take a long, hard look at the list. Notice anything? Yep, it's normally a summary of our own weak points! Recognise these and you'll suddenly open the flood-gates to easier discussions. Something to think about and something to act on.

Imagine you're trying to sell your car. To influence the potential purchaser, you'll need to notice whether they look at colours and feel the seats or whether they are interested in engine size.

Think about the person you want to influence. Let's assume you know them well – your mum, your boss … How do they influence themselves? How does your mum decide on something? She likes to stop; mull it over for a while. What about your boss? He likes to create a table of pros and cons. And your youngest sister, Rebecca? She'll be on the internet, checking out blogs and chat-rooms to see what 'real people' (as she puts it) think.

Your four-year-old, David, likes it when you sweep him up in your arms and influence with bounce and energy – the last thing he wants is a logical lecture. Funnily enough, though, that's just the way your six-year-old nephew likes to be handled – a nice 'adult' conversation.

All very well, you say, although it is true you hadn't quite thought about it like that before. But what about people you don't know? The used-car salesperson from whom you want two hundred off the price of that second-hand people-carrier. The jobsworth at the swimming pool who refuses to give your son a student-priced ticket. Well, idea 1: ask someone who knows them. Idea 2: try one way to communicate, then try another – write, then talk on the phone, then a face-to-face visit.

You can do this more formally if you like. Draw – yes, draw! – the faces of two people you want to influence: say, your mum over some of your career ideas and, say, the car salesperson about a price. Around each face write every way you know of that they are influenced. For instance, with your mum: mull it over, quiet cup of tea, what your dad says. With the used-car salesperson, the garage receptionist hinted that he might be more amenable if you could give him some leads to other business. Finally, turn those thoughts and comments into what you need to do:

Mum. Introduce the idea over a friendly chat and cup of tea. Mention a relevant article from *Hello* magazine and Dad's views. Leave it with her a few days.

Used-car salesperson. Tell him you could put his card up at the community centre with a flattering comment about how helpful he was in exchange for the extra discount.

'I did it my way.'
FRANK SINATRA – a powerful idea for all of us to try living up to

Defining idea...

11

Q **If I really don't know the person at all, aren't I bound to approach them in the wrong way and blow my chances totally?**

A   *You won't. It's never that final. This is just about upping the chances; enabling you to get a better result or an earlier result or both. Best thing is just to tread carefully – don't be too 'strong' in any way until you realise that they like to work in a particular manner.*

Q **How can I influence my publisher when she is so *totally* different to me? We don't see eye to eye on anything.**

A   *Difference can be good: it tends to spark new ideas. Also, it's possible that you actually agree; you're just coming at it from different angles. Keep listening and keep trying to understand her viewpoint. At some stage it will become a whole lot easier. Good places to start are to ask: Do they like to be influenced more logically or emotionally? Lots of detail or big picture? Quickly or with some reflection time? It's easy really once you work on her level.*

4

Take off your 'black hat'

You need to influence because there is something you do or don't want. However, don't be too quick to judge – maybe you don't understand the full situation yet.

Admit it: you've often been surprised when you've really got to know a person and truly understood why they seemed difficult. By reducing the number of such surprises, you'll be even better at having it your way.

Have you ever had a not-very-nice 'view' on a person – a newcomer to your business; a mum at the school when you're dropping off your children? Just a comment or their clothes or something caused you to form an unfavourable opinion of them. And then one day you got talking to them properly and found they were not at all as you had thought. You had misjudged them. Misjudging hinders our ability to influence somebody.

It happens to all of us – and, actually, for our self-preservation we are probably programmed to do it, so certainly don't feel bad about it. But of course it's not always that helpful when we are trying to change someone's thinking. Influencing

Here's an idea for you... **Try this mind game. Take a personal situation you want to influence; behaviour you want to change. Be very clear on how you 'think' about it at the moment. Consider all the details: what they say, what you say. Now 'flip it around'. Deliberately think the opposite. Okay, you don't believe it, but just experiment. So instead of thinking your dad is being deliberately obstructive, flip it around and think that he wants to help you. Try it!**

requires lots of options, flexibility and routes to where we are trying to get to. If we have prejudged someone, we may then only have one route – and that may not work.

A chap called Edward De Bono came up with a cool idea to help us with this. He said *pretend you are putting on a hat which causes you to think in a particular way*. He actually created six hats, but we really just need two.

First, there's the black hat. When you wear the black hat, you are looking at things in a logical and negative way ... what won't work. It's a pessimistic view. And there's the yellow hat. When you are wearing this hat you are looking at things in a logical but positive manner. You are being optimistic.

So, how do we use these hats? Well, think about some influencing you need to do:

■ Your girlfriend is not pulling her weight in doing the decorating.

■ Your boss is not helping your career, and he's meant to.

■ Your MP has said 'nothing can be done at the moment' about slowing driving speeds in your area of the city.

For each of these we're going to put on a black hat, then a yellow hat. If you really want to get into this (and, after all, you're not doing anything else at the moment are you?) then to add to the effect, wear the black hat when you are sitting in one part of the room and the yellow in another part of the room. And if you really, really want to get into this, find two real hats: one black and one yellow (but please, do this when nobody else is watching you!). Finally, put on gloomy music with the black hat (you'll know the one) and something really upbeat for the yellow hat.

Your girlfriend is not pulling her weight with the decorating. Black hat thinking: your girlfriend is lazy, clearly doesn't love you, and is taking advantage of your kindness. Yellow hat: she's working really hard at the moment and home is the only place she can recharge her batteries, plus you never criticise her and she really appreciates that. As you have never said anything about lending a hand, she assumes it's OK to put her feet up.

Your boss is not helping your career. Black hat thinking: he is deliberately holding you back because he is concerned you will be able to take his job. Yellow hat: he's working hard but doesn't want to give you false hope – he will mention something when it is a real opportunity.

Your MP has said nothing can be done about slowing speeds in your area. Black hat: he doesn't really care about the issue unless it is a vote winner. What's a couple of deaths a year? Yellow hat: he can't rush into this and must collect hard data to be able to argue the case properly.

'... **thinking is the ultimate human resource. Yet we can never be satisfied with our most important skill. No matter how good we become, we can become better.'**
EDWARD DE BONO, writer and lateral thinker

Defining idea...

How did
it go?

Q   **Isn't this hat business a bit artificial?**

A   *Yes! But that doesn't mean it's not useful. In a way it's deliberately artificial to cause a change in thinking. We're 'fooling' our brain to think in a different way. Try it and you will get into it.*

Q   **I'm getting the hang of these hats, but how can I get my neighbour into the idea? He's just so 'black hat' all of the time.**

A   *Keep talking to him and then, at an opportune time, simply say: 'maybe we should put our "yellow hats" on for a moment'. It may surprise and startle him into thinking differently when you explain. And when you say 'we' you're saying you accept you need to do it, too.*

5

He did *what*?
She actually said *that*?

Remember, you have rights. And they have rights. Some things are downright fundamental in any of your relationships, be it with your partner or with your bank.

Ensure you get those rights and support those rights by building them into your influencing. And respect the rights of others, too.

Just because we *can* influence somebody, is it reasonable for us to do so? You could try to influence your four-year-old into tidying up his room. But what's reasonable? That the room is immaculate? And if that *is* reasonable, is it healthy – or will it 'cramp' his creativity? You could influence your boyfriend into never going out drinking with his mates. But is that fair – or sensible?

These tricky questions about what is reasonable and fair will dictate how long-lasting our influencing is, whether it is worth attempting in the first place and the approach we might take. We may influence our toddler to tidy their room, but in the end they then never play with anything because it is too much hassle putting it all back. We may influence a supplier to give us a big discount but next year they don't even want to supply us because there are other clients who are more caring.

Think carefully about what rights are. They are fundamentals; givens. It helps the process of successful influencing hugely if they are understood and respected. For example: when influencing your new graduate team member, respect their inexperience; when influencing your manager, respect how busy she is; when influencing your granddad, respect his meandering ideas; when influencing your neighbour, respect his lawn worries; when influencing your teenage daughter, respect the 'loves of her life'; when influencing your bank manager, respect his financial expertise; when influencing your restaurant owner, respect his desire to close on time.

We may influence our boyfriend to stop going out drinking but in the end he finds himself a new girlfriend.

Try this out. Who are you trying to influence at the moment? Let's go for a walk. No, not to see them! Just to plan our approach. While walking, let's think.

Say you want to influence Zoë's biology teacher. Why? Well, because Zoë needs biology if she is to become a vet and she has previously enjoyed biology. However, this year she isn't, and you think it's because of her teacher's style. You'd like the teacher to be a bit more 'gentle' with Zoë. Okay, we're clear on that. We'll come back to it in a minute. Keep walking.

You also need to get your really good friend Tim to stop turning up on your doorstep at odd hours wanting to go for a drink. You have moved on from that lifestyle now you are married.

And you need to influence the bank to extend your overdraft for another six months – and this is after they said the last extension was *absolutely* it.

Wow, you have got a lot on! Keep walking and see if you can work out the 'rights' on both sides of the discussion. Then see if you agree with the ones suggested here.

Zoë's biology teacher has a right to maintain discipline in the class, which may restrict her flexibility of style. But Zoë does have a right to a good 'working' relationship with her teacher, so maybe the thing to aim for is a one-to-one meeting where Zoë and her teacher meet and talk. Then, as Zoë feels she now 'understands' her teacher, she won't find her style so intimidating in the classroom.

As for Tim, he does have a right to be treated with kindness – there's a good long-standing friendship going on there. But you do have a right (and your partner, too, of course) not to be bothered by Tim at odd hours. And you have a right to move on. So, be polite, and be persistent, but explain to Tim that your friendship is going to have to move into a new phase with different activities that are planned in advance.

Much as many of us hate our banks, they do have a right to get us to behave professionally and sensibly. Although you do have the right to ask for support, they have a right to say no. So, probably the best strategy is to simply ask the bank: 'What do I need to do to get the overdraft extension?' The answer will probably be something to do with increasing their confidence. It's probably best not to threaten to go to another bank – the new bank will most likely work in much the same way.

'Example is not the main thing in influencing others. It is the only thing.'
ALBERT SCHWEITZER, philosopher and medical missionary

Defining idea...

Easy enough really, isn't it? And you'll find that thinking it through while walking or cooking or taking your morning swim works very well.

Q   **Nobody's perfect. We all make mistakes. Do we lose credibility at that point?**

A   *Certainly not. As a new team leader at the school canteen, you clearly want to influence through the way you are and behave. But if you make a mistake – and you will – then simply apologise. The ability to admit you got it wrong and say you're sorry is showing your strength as a leader and you are still influencing. You cannot know everybody's 'rights' immediately.*

Q   **How do I know what is fair in a particular situation?**

A   *We can never be sure. But follow your head and follow your heart. Most of us, deep down, know what is appropriate in a particular situation. You can always ask for time to think. You can always apologise – in the early stage, thereby showing that you can always change your mind.*

6

No, not now! Get your timing right

Here's an idea that's very easy, very potent and yet often forgotten: choose the right time. There's a right time for everything, isn't there? So too if you want to have it your way.

It won't help your influencing if those you wish to influence are tired, stressed, getting ready to go out or wanting to watch the latest episode of The Simpsons.

You need to pick the right time for the targets of your influencing, not just a time that suits you. That's it. It's as simple as that. Admit it, though: you'd not really given it much thought, had you?

As you know, emotions are powerful things, so when that old lady allows her dog to go digging in your garden, you want to shout at her *now*. When your son Vipul gets home with critical red ink all over the essay you gave ten out of ten last night, you want to give his head teacher an ear-bashing *now*. And when the builder leaves old timber in the driveway and it punctures a tyre on your Mini Cooper as you return home, you want to sack him – *now*.

Relax with a cup of your favourite tea or coffee. Now, this person you need to influence. When is he or she at their best? Are they a morning or an evening kind of person? Do they like to 'clear their desk' before they talk to you? Or is lunchtime good for them? Or when the kids have gone to bed – or is that the worst time because they see that as their 'own' time? Possibly the weekend? Whenever it is, that's when you are going to have the conversation.

But – and it's a big BUT – 'now' is probably not the best time: we are not going to get the result we wanted. We are going to get a very upset old lady and look like a horrible bully. If we shout at the head teacher, it will only backfire on Vipul. As for sacking the builder, that'd be crazy. At least he turns up, works to budget and is polite; you want a clear drive, too?

Remember too that if it's not the best time for that somebody else then they will probably not be listening to you. And if they aren't listening, you are not going to influence. And if you can't influence, you can't get what you want. Here are some classic bad times to avoid:

Too soon: 'Hang on, I haven't even got my coat off yet!'

Too late: 'Look, can we talk about this tomorrow? I really need to get off home – now.'

When they are too distracted: 'Okay, but I've got a lot on at the moment. Couldn't we do this another time, maybe?'

When they are on the way to a meeting: 'I can give you *one* minute!'

When neither of you has had time to reflect: 'I can't believe you just said that!'

At the end of a busy day: 'Look, I've had a tough day with an evil boss and idiot clients, and my laptop's stopped working. I am really not going to listen to you table-thumping about how we should be recycling more.'

When you are too emotional: 'Where the bl**dy hell have you been?'

When they do not have enough time to respond: 'Hang on. I've got a presentation to give in 45 minutes.'

When it simply isn't fair: 'Look, I've just been made redundant myself. Can't we talk about this tomorrow?'

The aim should always be to find a time when the other person will be receptive and have a bit of time to reflect and discuss. Given the pace of life today, that's going to be difficult but, if you can't find the right time, the danger is that your whole argument will probably be ignored.

'Who has time? Who has time? But then if we never take time, how can we have time?'
THE MEROVINGIAN, *Matrix Reloaded*

Defining idea...

Q **I am angry *now* and this needs to be sorted *now*. So, why shouldn't I go for it?**

A *Agreed, the issue does need to be sorted. However, what you want is a successful resolution to this issue and your girlfriend is too exhausted from her business trip for you to make any real progress. So, use your anger to prepare. Jot down ideas and avoid a shouting match. You know it makes sense! It often seems that 'time is of the essence' and 'there is no time like now', but pick the right time and the results will be worth it. You can do it in one of two ways: either apparently 'spontaneously' talk to them at that right time (which would probably be best for most of our 'personal' influencing situations) or we could 'book' that time (which may well be better for our business situations).*

Q **There is *never* a good time with my boss: he's basically always in a bad mood. So, what do I do with him?**

A *You are probably right, but think about it a little more. It's a very unusual person who doesn't have some time when they are more approachable. How about the beginning of a new month when good sales figures are in? Or just before lunch when he reckons he's done a good morning's work? Those are good times aren't they? Anything that makes a person listen to you properly and take it seriously has got to be good for having your own way.*

7

Choose the right place

It won't help your influencing if there isn't the right level of privacy or quietness. The supermarket is probably not a good place to discuss why nobody – except you – puts the bins out.

This is really about mood-making — how to create a perfect ambiance for influencing. Have you ever tried to seduce someone? Of course you have, so you can see what we're getting at.

Low lights, candles, romantic music ... walks by the beach ... best club in town – you were doing a special form of influencing we know as seduction. And you certainly gave thought to the place.

Of course, some 'seductions' are done gazing at a sunset or while enjoying a beautiful picnic, or maybe after a loud rock concert, but they are all about place. Place has a huge impact on your success rate of changing someone's thinking.

Although it seems obvious, think about why you don't try to seduce someone on a busy high street or in an airport lounge – unless you're desperate and it is your only opportunity, of course!

Here's an idea for you... Think about the influencing you need to do. If it were you, where would you like to be influenced? Is it business, and it would therefore be nice to talk over a pleasant meal as they are trying to persuade you into taking a job with them? Or would a walk in the park do the trick with your young daughter? Or over an ice-cream with your teenage son after the latest James Bond film? Or maybe in the board room, to show you are special? Wherever *you* would like to be influenced gives you a very strong clue as to where *they* would like to be influenced.

The reason 'place' is important when influencing is because it has a big impact on our mood – on how we feel. And mood will dictate how easy it is to influence or not. Generally, we want to put someone into a mood that makes them more receptive to other ideas, open to thoughts that they can change and generally make them feel good.

Here are things about place that help positive mood-making:

- *Light:* signifies clarity and we all like to feel we know what we are doing.
- *Space:* we like to feel we can 'stretch'; that we are not being confined in our thinking.
- *Warmth:* if we are too cold, we are thinking only about one thing – how to get warm.
- *Comfort:* if the chair feels odd we can't give the discussion a full 100%.
- *Positive colours:* uplifting 'sunny' colours tend to work better, but mainly in subdued hues.
- *Easy to talk, but not silence:* that's why a café or restaurant can work, particularly if there is plenty of room between tables.

- *Energy:* a walk can create pace and energy, just like the lively café as just mentioned.
- *Privacy:* with very delicate matters, a booked meeting room will guarantee privacy and encourage discussion.

And of course, there are things that can bring the mood down:

- *Darkness/gloom:* in bleak meeting rooms full of trailing cables and empty coffee cups, you're making it a whole lot harder to influence the client.
- *Poor lighting:* (as opposed to low or discreet lighting) this feels too much like a battle zone.
- *Barriers:* this is an important one in business – get out from behind the big desk, and make sure chairs are the same sizes.

A bit of thought can ensure that when you start your conversation and you begin to discuss what you want or what is troubling you, your friend or colleague is already receptive simply because of the environment in which they find themselves. In many environments, the comfort is further enhanced by 'comfort food and/or drink': a good cup of coffee, a nice lunch or a glass of wine. Although, of course, it is worth taking care with alcohol – you really want the person to feel they made the decision themselves rather than the six shots of vodka inside them.

'Location, location, location.'
ANON

Defining
idea...

How did it go?

Q **This is all very well but I don't have an office, and meeting rooms are always in use for group sessions rather than one-to-ones. So, how do I get 'the right place' – how do I get privacy?**

A   *You're thinking along the right lines. Without privacy, you can't really get someone to talk honestly. And, without that, it's difficult to really work out some kind of agreement that's good for both of you. Here are some ideas for you. Firstly, could you borrow a colleague's office when he/she is out? It gives you a door you can close and hence privacy. Secondly, in good weather, why not go outside and take a walk – just as they do in all the good spy films? Nobody can hear you and you have complete privacy. Or you could head out to a coffee shop at a quiet time.*

Q **Are there any guidelines concerning what makes for a good environment for selling?**

A   *Selling is, of course, a very special form of influencing. So, what kind of room should you be looking for? If it's an office, ensure that there is a simple 'break out' circular table around which you can sit rather than facing each other across a desk. (Huge desks create an unnecessary barrier, as you will realise.) If it's a meeting room, try to ensure it's tidy but also not too 'stark' – essentially one that 'lifts the mood' and makes people feel more optimistic and positive about what is happening. Such rooms tend to have natural light, pale furniture, and are not too cramped. It's worth tidying a room and even getting rid of some furniture (temporarily!) if it is a very important session. If it is a conference with lots of PowerPoint slides, think very carefully about what the room looks like and how it encourages people to behave when the lights 'come up'.*

8

Have a plan – and use it

Think it through. Even better, write it down. Where will you start? Where do you want to end up? What will happen along the way? Here's how to create a great plan; one that works.

You wouldn't cook a special meal without a plan, would you? Would you go for the world's best job without a plan? Would you go hiking in and on the Western Isles of Scotland without a plan?

Well, you certainly shouldn't. Why not? Because you want to be successful, that's why! You want the meal to be special, you want to get the job and you don't want to get lost in the wilderness.

A plan helps you to be successful. When you create a plan, you think it through: 'I will say that, then he will say this. I'll explain why I want the rent lowered and he will mutter something about prices going up for building materials. And I will respond with ….' When you create a plan you also look at what might go wrong: 'He may start shouting, in which case I will say "look: think it through and get back to me".' 'Or she may say "who's going to …?", in which case …'

Here's an idea for you... **Consider what a good plan certainly will have. It's similar to a story: it has a start (how you will start the whole thing off: *'Pete, I know you probably don't want this conversation, but we need to talk about money ...'*), a middle (how will you begin to get into detail: *'great, so we've agreed we're both mismanaging our finances; what about this ... as a practical way forward?'*) and an end (the action plan: *'cool; so you will ... and I will ...'*). Create the story (start, middle and end) for that bit of influencing you urgently need to do and you'll find you have a plan. And it will be a lot easier to produce than most plans.**

When you create a plan, ensure you prepare everything to the best of your ability: your notes, the evidence, the article from the newspaper about salary scales. When you plan, see you also have a back-up – plan B. When you plan, you have something to look at if you lose your track.

Convinced? You should be!

However, it's possible you've got a few concerns, too – such as you hate planning! Bit of a nuisance, that. However, that's why we're talking about one, simple plan – not planning – and it will be easy to accomplish.

You might voice some other concerns such as: 'doesn't a plan restrict you?' Well, no, having a plan doesn't cause you to lose your spontaneity. Having a plan enables you to unleash your true spontaneity and creativity.

Think about the next influencing you need to do. Grab a bit of paper and write down the answers to these questions. Write quickly – that's important to making this process painless. Don't particularly think about it: just write. We're going to be using parts of your brain that know exactly what to do if we trust them.

■ What do you really want from this influencing conversation?
What would success look like? Feel like? Sound like?

■ What would you be willing to accept if you couldn't get it all?
What is your back-up plan?

■ What would be a good time to have the conversation?
Breakfast? Lunch? Supper? After work? During a work-out at the gym?

■ What would be a good place to have the discussion?
In the car? At the beach? In the Italian coffee bar?

■ Where's your evidence and argumentation (the stuff will help you convince the other person)?
Have you got a copy of that?

■ What are they likely to say?
Great! Get stuffed! Sounds cool to me! You must be joking! Possibly.

■ How are they likely to act?
Positive. Cheerful. Sulky. Depressed. Hurt.

'**To achieve great things, two things are needed: a plan, and not quite enough time.**'
LEONARD BERNSTEIN, US conductor and composer

Defining idea...

■ How will you respond?
Resourceful. Unsure.

■ Who could you practise with to ensure you have got it all correct?
Gerry from sales. Lucy at the toddler group.

31

How did it go?

Q **What can you say to convince me I'm wrong to hate planning? I think it's limiting. I prefer to just go with the flow.**

A *You're entitled to that view but if you do not have a plan then you may not be able to do your best 'go with the flow' work. Influencing is not black and white. This idea works and is here to help. 'Going with the flow' does not exclude a good plan. Armed with a plan, your flow will continue to go in a compelling direction. All you have to do is write down your ideas, and do it very quickly, then stop. That means we don't get into planning for planning's sake.*

Q **What happens if it becomes clear within minutes that you have a plan that isn't appropriate?**

A *Some might say it wasn't a very good plan, then, was it? However, that's not at all helpful. To be fair, this can happen. However, look at it as a good learning experience – maybe you didn't put as much thought into the plan as would have been useful. And, of course, it's still all right, because part of your plan was your back-up plan B, wasn't it? Just teasing! Seriously, if your plan doesn't work, plan more next time. There's always a next time and every time you'll get better at having it your way.*

9

You might need to act, so rehearse

Tricky conversations are much easier when we've said it all before. Practise as you are driving to meet your boss; say everything you need to get off your chest.

As they say, practice makes perfect. However, that's not going to be helpful advice when you may only have one chance at the real thing — and you don't want to mess it up.

When you have been in a situation before, you tend to handle it better. Remember your first trip to the bank manager's office after you'd just started your business? Yes: your nervousness showed, but you're much more confident these days. Remember your first date? How about your first driving lesson? You were hardly at your best in those two situations, understandably.

Here's an idea for you... **You need about twenty minutes alone in a room. Think about the influencing situation you will be in. Now stand or sit, and practise saying what you need to say. You'll probably find your mobile phone has a simple record facility, so try recording yourself and see how it sounds. If a long wall mirror is available, that would be brilliant. Stand taller/sit taller and notice how much more confident you feel. Perhaps you should practise the opening hand-shake if it's a commercial situation you face – hold your body as you will hold your body when you have the interview for the director's job.**

Here's the sort of challenge we're talking about:

- one meeting with the MP to get the speed reduced from 50 to 20 in your local area

- one meeting with the farmer about his cattle wandering into your garden at night

- one chance to get the neighbours to cut down the overhanging branch

- one chance to get an injection of capital for our business expansion

- one chance to convince the HR director of the viability of our job-share proposal.

We have got to get it right, and get it right first time.

So, we will do the next best thing to having done it before: we will do what good actors do – rehearse. A top actor wouldn't go out on stage expecting it to go well without rehearsal. A football team would not expect to play a tough game brilliantly without some practice training. Why should we be different? If our brain and body have been there before, we are much more likely to be successful. We need to rehearse what we're going to say, how we are going to move, how we are going to react. And we can do that at almost any time: so let's start.

As mentioned, we need to rehearse two main things: words and body. It's best to practise them separately at first and then combine them as in a real meeting.

Firstly, words. With words, think about which word/s you will use. For example, you want a 'market rate' (a nice neutral, non-emotional commercial term) for your salary rather than 'a bl**dy decent salary increase'. Or 'more time to plan' rather than 'fewer tasks thrown at me'. Then think about the tone you use. Use a tone that sounds 'can do' rather than 'complaining'; 'professional' rather than 'little girl' or 'laddish'.

Secondly, body. Start with great maintained eye contact and support that with an 'open' body language (no folded arms); top it up with standing up or sitting up straight as appropriate.

Now, bring the two together. Imagine coming out of the lift. Waiting in the MD's reception area. Getting up gracefully. Shaking hands. Declining, politely, with a smile, a cup of coffee. Sitting comfortably on the slippery leather sofa. Making good eye contact and sharing a few pleasantries before easily moving into some 'serious concerns you have about the way female managers are treated in the company', opening your notebook and quoting a few facts. Stay open when the MD's language and tone become dismissive. Stand up and move to his white-board to explain things in more detail and allow you a stronger body language position. Look him in the eyes in a non-hostile manner but insist on some follow-through action.

Defining idea...

'Acting is not about being emotional, but being able to express emotion.'
KATE REID, actor with the Royal Shakespeare Company

How did it go?

Q **At school my drama teacher told me 'you can't act to save your life!'. So, what hope is there for me? Does that mean I won't make a good influencer?**

A *It's pretty safe to ignore much of what was said to you at school! And you know that deep down don't you? They didn't really know you. Many teachers were pretty negative about many of the kids. So, don't read any deep (or slight!) significance into an unfair comment made years ago. After all, if you weren't able to act back then, that suggests someone's teaching wasn't brilliant! You can act, just as anyone can if they put their mind to it. And we don't need you to do Shakespeare, just you.*

Q **But if I'm acting, doesn't that mean I'm not really being me?**

A *Good question. You're clearly confused here. This is not about acting and becoming someone else (as, granted, real actors often have to do.) No, this is acting to be the best version of you – the you that is polite but persistent, focused yet sensitive, firm but flexible, smiley yet tough. You know the one: that version of you that can win!*

10

What to do if it goes awry

Actually the aim is to make damn sure it doesn't! However, in keeping with health and safety thinking, it's better to be safe than sorry. And accidents *do* happen.

If the worst does happen and everything you had hoped for just disappears in a cloud of emotion or incorrect facts (or both), you need to know exactly how to remedy the situation.

You've thought it through carefully, you've planned it out and you've rehearsed this careful, mature, one-to-one conversation. And then on the day they ask you to do a presentation instead. Given that all your influencing had been planned via dialogue, this is not good.

You'd Googled and got amazing data from three different sources which proved how you were underpaid. Then, on the day, they pulled out a *Financial Times* supplement from that very morning which showed how salaries for your position were actually dropping again.

On the day you were going to convince her to marry you, you lose your voice.

Here's an idea for you...

Collar a good friend because you're going to play a great game called 'extreme influencing': *what's the worst that could happen ... and how would you handle it?* **It's not for the faint-hearted.**

Player A: state any influencing situation (e.g. salary negotiation; feud with neighbour; trying to convince a parking attendant to let you off the ticket). Big or small, it doesn't matter: any situation will do.

Player B: state the worst possible outcome.

Player B: state a disaster (e.g. arrived late for the wedding and need to convince person mowing lawn to allow you to park in their drive for 45 minutes).

Player A: state how you would cope.

These things happen. All things being equal, if you use a few brilliant ideas, they probably will not happen too often, but one reader, somewhere, every so often, is going to find their best laid plans have gone to pot. So, we must do what we can to make sure they can cope.

Here's what to do. Don't pretend nothing has gone wrong if it obviously has; don't pretend to know something when you don't. Once you've acknowledged that things have gone pear-shaped, you need to re-take control and move on. For instance: '... actually, no, I wasn't aware that had been a recent policy decision. May I ask why you are so firmly against the principle of job-sharing?'

Assume there is another way – there always is: 'I'm texting this because I've lost my voice. That gives me another reason why I'll always remember this day! Will you marry me?'

Apologise: 'I'm sorry: clearly those figure do not fully justify the reason I'm asking for a project delay. That is my error.'

Ask for another opportunity: 'I am aware the board meets again on Thursday; would you be kind enough to give me 10 minutes then?'

Show that this is not something that could have been anticipated, despite your scrupulous attention to detail: 'Clearly something is telling us to take an early lunch: I can't remember a time in all my career as an account manager when two laptops have gone down. While we are having lunch, my colleagues will get the demonstration ready. We won't let you go home without a decision, gentlemen!'

Keep it 'light': 'Well guys. It had to happen to me one day. All my slides have been killed by a virus and I've left my back-up in the hotel, which is an hour away in this morning traffic. But I'm pleased, anyway, because I was looking for an excuse to talk to you about ...'

Keep everyone informed: 'We *will* be going ahead – it's just that the room has been double-booked.'

Compensate if you can: 'Although we were here to ask for our own common room and you have been kind enough to grant that request, we are very sorry about the chaotic way in which we presented the survey data. So, the cappuccinos are on us!'

Note that the way you handle these 'disasters' will in its own way make you a stronger or weaker influencer. Talk calmly, with authority and explain what you will do to remedy the situation.

'You should treat all disasters as if they were trivialities but never treat a triviality as if it were a disaster.'
QUENTIN CRISP

Defining idea...

How did it go?

Q It's really frustrating for me. However hard I prepare, at tough points in the conversation, I blush. Surely, that's a real disaster for me, isn't it?

A *Not necessarily. Some people blush, some people don't; girls tend to do so a bit more than men; younger people more often than older ones. Don't try to stop it: you can't. Although it's hard to do, just accept the fact: work with it – it's part of you, like your height or skin colour. If you make sure your influencing skills are good, nobody will even notice the odd blush and that is a fact. Don't stop blushing, start influencing!*

Q I'm so nervous about this: I've got just one chance to convince the manager that this job-share will work and I know it's going to go wrong. What can I do?

A *Let's sort out one thing right now – stop saying to yourself, 'I know it's going to go wrong'. Things have a horrid habit of being self-fulfilling with that kind of talk! The game we are playing here is that if we use one or two brilliant ideas, then failure's highly unlikely. And if we play 'extreme influencing', we'll probably be able to anticipate what might go wrong. Finally, you are a smart person – believe it – so you will think of something. It's going to be okay!*

11

Get an outsider's view

Sometimes you are simply too close to the subject to do yourself justice. Someone else's perspective might just give you the balanced view you need, so keep an open mind.

An outsider can restore the clarity of your thinking by looking at your problem with a fresh pair of eyes unblinkered by the minutiae. In important situations, it's worth asking a professional adviser for help.

You know what it's like when you're going round and round in circles. How's it best to convince your boyfriend to sell his lovely Morris Minor? On the one hand, it is beautiful and you love it, plus it's easy to fix it yourselves if there are problems and most people really admire it. On the other hand, though, it can't cope with today's motorways and it's beginning to be infuriatingly unreliable. You've had three cups of tea trying to work out a way forward. Meanwhile you've also done a pros-and-cons list four times and it's still not helping.

During the past week, you've tried all your favourite problem-crunching techniques: going for a walk; having a swim; scoffing some chocolate (actually, a lot); and you

Get clear about that intractable difficulty again. How will you influence your boyfriend to sell his Morris Minor? How will you get the landlord to tackle the rats in the roof? How will you tackle your boss about the lack of bonus this quarter, or the local church about your pagan wedding plans? And now recognise you are stuck. If you were to get advice from someone, who would be best – most brutal with you? That's the person you need to use. Okay, you don't really want to discuss it with them because the advice they will give may well be too close to the truth, but they will be best.

even rang your mum. Nothing helped. How on earth will you convince him that the car's *got* to go?

The good news is we can help you, and we can help you a lot. You will probably not get out of your loop without an injection of fresh thinking. It's known as *advice*.

You didn't like that term, did you? You know best. Your boyfriend is a nuisance with his passion for ancient cars, whereas you're much more sensible with your three-year-old French hatch-backs. Your landlord is a scoundrel and you are the perfect tenant. Your art gallery will eventually make money ... it's just a matter of time. Yeah, yeah, but hang on just a moment – what if advice would help? And there's the thing – *what if?*

You do feel strongly about this matter, and you probably do know best, but maybe, just maybe, you are too close to the subject. It's a possibility, isn't it?

Believe it – an outsider's view is helpful. When you think you've looked at every option, you can benefit from a fresh perspective. That's what another person can do for you. And you need an open mind to just consider this alternative view – does it have any validity? Think about where you are:

- *You're emotionally too 'wound up' by it all.* An alternative view will detect when too much emotion is perhaps swaying your thinking and, therefore, your influencing ability.
- *You're far too close to the trees to be able to see the wood.* A good outsider will pull you back and will lift you up to the helicopter view: what's going on here?
- *You're sick of it all.* It's not that you expect the other person to solve the problem you have, but if they could just get you thinking about it again, that would be helpful.
- *You need some hints.* How on earth do you decide how to structure a bonus scheme? You've searched a bit on the net but that doesn't help and your first salesperson will be arriving soon to negotiate his selling package. You don't want to lose him but nor do you want to pay him too much ... aaargh!
- *You have tried everything.* There's always one more idea, and an outsider will have it. As irritating as you might find it, this is absolutely true.

A professional adviser's view can also be invaluable. Recognise the situation and get help. Maybe just a one-hour session will be all you need.

- When anything gets to an apparent point of no return – divorce, no way to pay the debts and fundamental disagreements about schooling for the children.
- When you need an independent arbiter, a professional will tell you, for instance, how much would be a fair split.
- When you need some legal advice. Can you just sack her? Better find out!

Defining idea...

'Advice is what we ask for when we already know the answer but wish we didn't.'
ERICA JONG, author and poet

Q **How do I find someone who can give me good, reliable advice?**

A *Consider someone who has experience in the appropriate area (if you have a business difficulty, how about that couple at the gym who managed to rebuild their business after bankruptcy?) or who is very thoughtful (if you have a relationship issue, how about your friend at the Women's Institute?) or who is a good listener (your mentor at work). Whoever it is, approach them at a good time, give them a quick view of the challenge you have, and then ask them if they will consider helping you. It's best if you don't have to twist their arms too much – a reluctant adviser is not always particularly helpful.*

Q **Aren't 'professional' advisers always prohibitively expensive for people with limited financial means?**

A *It depends what you mean by expensive. Of course, they must charge for their time and it could prove unlikely they can help you in just one session. However, if they come well recommended, they should be able to give you a decent return on your investment by helping you solve your problem in the best way. Think of the potential down-side: if this influencing issue is not solved soon, what is it going to cost you in the long term?*

12

Pretend to get an outsider's view

We've agreed that an outsider's perspective can be invaluable in guiding our influencing strategy. We now need to know what to do when that 'impartial view' isn't there for us.

You've sorted out a few situations over the years and you consider yourself pretty good at influencing. One thing you have learnt is that, although you don't like it, external advice usually helps a lot.

An important lesson for any successful influencer is that it can be immensely helpful to put your pride aside for a moment and take on board the views of other people. The trouble is that there are times when there won't be anybody around to help you out.

Here's an idea for you...

Place three chairs in a triangle. Set them out so that two chairs directly face each another and the third one is 'observing'. Chair one is going to be you – you at your best. Chair two is the person you are trying to influence and chair three is an impartial 'person in the street'. Next, think through your influencing situation. Firstly, sit in chair one (you at your best): what do you think is the best thing to convince him/her? Then sit in chair two and think as the person you wish to influence. What is he/she really looking for? Sit in chair three and look at the situation as an external impartial adviser would. What might they suggest?

Say you're travelling and your whole itinerary has been screwed. You're making no progress with your travel firm and you are wondering what the next step is. What's your best strategy for influencing them?

Or, while on a business trip, you get a long message from your girlfriend saying she wants to 'pack in' the relationship 'for the sake of her career' but you're 99% sure it's simply because the recent pressure of the 'big deal' negotiations has stressed her out. How can you get her to reconsider?

Or, your publisher wants to pulp one of your books that is finally gaining some momentum. How can you get them to see the error of their ways?

Sounds like you might need some advice, but who are you going to ask? Don't worry – you are going to get help. You see, there are real advisers and there are virtual advisers. Real advisers are great, of course, but when they are not available, virtual advisers are in many ways better because they're on call 24/7.

So, where do you get your virtual advisers from? The answer lies in the depths of your brain – your imagination. Let's set up your virtual team; your dream team.

If you were able to have anyone to give you advice, who would it be? They can be dead or alive. They charge no fees and they're available on demand. So, who would you choose? Richard Branson, perhaps? Gandhi; your dad; your primary school head teacher; Mick Jagger; Jane Austen; the bloke who spoke to you at that conference; Sally your mate who has started her own salon? You get the picture. Go on: pick who would be in your team.

As you consider your team you might want to think about the various skills that would be useful to have: a strategic thinker, a pragmatist, a lateral thinker, a financial wizard, a relationships guru.

Now you've got your squad, what do you do with them? Well, you use them as you would a real team: ask them for advice. When you have an influencing challenge and you need some help and inspiration, just say, for instance:

- What would Richard Branson say in this situation?

- What would my old primary school teacher have suggested?

'Some people like my advice so much that they frame it upon the wall rather than using it.'
GORDON DICKSON, painter and sculptor

Defining idea...

To increase the benefit and make the advice even more robust, use the self-discipline of writing down the expert's view. For example, 'Richard Branson advises that I should change my bank, but also take a lot of reasons along to the bank as to why I will be a very attractive customer to have long-term.'

For this to offer practical benefits to you it's vital to suspend any doubts you have. Open your mind and try it – because it works!

How did
it go?

Q   Isn't this pretending just kidding yourself?

A   Only if you think it is. The mind is amazing: allow its power to run by just assuming the virtual team process will work, and it will. Spend time deciding who would be good to have on your team. Take a moment and consider what they would advise. And that funny little exercise with the chairs: have you tried that yet? That'll really stretch your imagination, but you'll find it really does work. Your mind will be focused and ideas will develop.

Q   What should I do if I can't think of anyone to be my virtual adviser?

A   Then leave it a while and come back to it. You are possibly too close to everything. What would be good is to step back from the influencing challenge and look at how you are going to make progress from different angles. That's where your team comes in. You will be able to think of a team, you just need a bit of time. Remember also that there is nothing to stop you just picking a name out of the newspaper – you simply need a bit of familiarity with the person. And then you say, so what would the mayor of London say? What would the chairman of the school's committee say? It's the 'jolt' of thinking in a different way that's so very useful.

13

Keep trying

The more important the influencing, the longer it may well take. Keep trying and keep trying in different ways. Your tenacity will pay off.

In a long-term influencing challenge, as well as never giving up, it's important to come at the problem with an evolving armoury of different approaches.

It simply isn't working. You sat down after supper to talk to your son about his lack of revision for his exams and one or two other issues and the discussion went absolutely nowhere. In fact it probably made things even worse.

You thought it would be a simple 'drop-in' discussion at the dry-cleaner's about the stain they have *added* to your jacket. But the discussion rapidly became an argument and went nowhere.

And you are absolutely passionate about climate change but, although many different groups are making the right noises, who is actually getting anything done?

Here's an idea for you...

Who do you currently need to influence? The local council. About what? You want a bigger recycling bin but you don't feel you should have to pay for it. So, think what your first approach is going to be. It could be just you on your own, ringing them up. But be persistent – try a few times. What's your second approach if you get a definite and absolute no? Talk to that person's boss. And if that doesn't work? Get the local paper involved. Three different approaches. That's The Three Threes Rule.

And then there's the man of your dreams who's just arrived in the area. But does he pay you any attention? Has he even noticed you yet? How are you going to influence him?

What do you do in situations such as these? Persist? Give up? Well, you certainly shouldn't give up – certainly not until you have tried a few times anyway!

Granted, there are some influencing situations that are 'quick-fix', like the wrong arithmetic on the paper bill or the friendly neighbours about the damage their son did to your fence. But some influencing takes time. Don't rush it. It'll be worth it when it's done, and most likely it will stick, too.

So, we do persist, but do we keep trying the same message? Remember that, just like you, most people are busy, so we have to keep pushing and we have to get through the daily 'noise' and distractions until they finally listen to what we are saying. And we have to try different methods because sometimes one method simply does not work with one particular person. Hence we keep trying and change our approach until it fits the bill.

Sometimes, time is the only thing that's stopping us from doing some fantastic influencing: time for the idea to be fully absorbed, time for the idea to be understood; time for us to explain it to them properly. That's why persistence is so essential.

It cannot be stressed how powerful simple persistence is. But do remember, persistence is about energy and keeping the focus on your overall aim (of getting the salary increase, the rent reduction, the council to reduce road speeds). It doesn't necessarily mean you keep repeating the same message (which can simply be really annoying).

- When somebody says no, they actually mean *not now*, so ask them when would be a good time.

- When somebody says they don't like that idea, what they actually mean is that *they haven't given it enough consideration.* Write it down, send it to them and follow-up with a phone call.

- When somebody says they're not sure you are the right person, what they mean is *they don't understand your full value.* Explain the idea to them again, but this time ensure you get 100% attention.

- When somebody says that's a stupid idea, what they mean is *they're frightened of that idea.* Explain it to them again, but with added reassurance.

- When somebody says it's too late, what they really mean is *they don't know how we do it at this late stage.* Explain to them how it can be done.

Oh, and stay polite. Nobody will be able to turn you down if you stay polite. Polite and persistent: that's a magic formula.

'A winner never stops trying.'
VINCENT LOMBARDI, American
football coach

Defining
idea...

How did it go?

Q **How will I know when it's the right time to try a different way?**

A *When you have tried several times and you are convinced the other person understands the message, but it's not worked. Then you need to try another message or a different context. Remember, sometimes the message is okay, but it's the wrong context. For example, if you are trying to influence your husband to buy a bigger house but he is concerned about a bigger mortgage this close to retirement, how about giving the same message but in the show house? Then your message will have more impact.*

Q **Are there any circumstances when I'll have to acknowledge that I should give up altogether?**

A *There are some things you will never want to give up on: influencing on social injustice, for example. It may take years but when the road speeds are finally reduced, what a breakthrough for you and other parents of young children in the area. However, with others, there comes a point where maybe we do have to accept that it is simply not going to be. If there's another keen bidder, you are just not going to get that house at the price you want; you're not going to be asked to be the manager of the Paris office if there's somebody more qualified for the post. Be realistic – let it go and move on. You probably can't win them all! Remember, there's lots of other exciting influencing to be done in life.*

14

Aim high

Go for something you really, *really* want and you'll learn skills that will give you an excellent chance of having it your way.

Of course, have some back-up positions and be willing to be flexible, but certainly start with aiming high: a salary increase, the guaranteed parking spot, the home-on-time issue.

Get a clear picture of what you really want and – assuming it is within the bounds of reality and legality, of course – stick to that initially. Eventually you may need to dilute your 'demands' or expectations a little, but don't lower the bar too soon. After all, there's little harm in asking and you may get the right result.

There are many challenges in the world of influencing (and that's why we're providing lots of brilliant ways to manage these challenges). One of these is certainly to ensure that we get our target right in the first place. You see, if we aim too low we may regret it for a long time. Whatever initial salary we get at the interview will set the pace for all future salary increases; whatever cleaning and tidying arrangements we set with our flatmates will become immutable.

Take a seat. A really comfortable seat where you can put your head back a bit would be especially good. Now close your eyes and think about this influencing you need to do. Bring to mind the situation and just dream a bit. What would be great? What would you really like to happen? Dreaming a little to set your sights will work wonders for your ability to influence.

And that's why it's worth aiming high – we can't ramp things up but we can always come down a bit. Also, if we ask 'high', we are positioning ourselves as valuable and confident. However, a word of caution: if we ask for too much, we might be seen as too expensive, arrogant or simply too greedy.

If we ask the landlord for a whole lot of changes then we may get the one we really want: a new shower installed. But perhaps he might just think we are an unreasonable tenant and do the one cheapest thing he can do: fix the broken kitchen window. He may even not renew our tenancy!

So, what do we do? Well, one thing to bear in mind is that, so far, we have assumed that things are black and white – that we can either have one thing or the other and that we will either have success or not. In reality of course, there is some middle ground. With a bit of skill, though – which you'll certainly have from practising these ideas – we can assure the best possible outcome.

Thus, we could ask for a 12% increase over our current salary but when the boss balks at that we could counter by being willing to take a little less as long as there is an agreement to re-review in six months rather than the normal twelve. We can ask for the new shower but if the response really is a no, then let's get the window fixed and come back to the shower at a later date.

And, by the way, how do we know what 'aiming high' is? How do we know what salaries are possible? What rent reduction we might achieve? Here, research is the key: on the web, from people in the local authorities, asking our MP, talking to others in our situation who have got it their way. One of the many great things about the web is how much information is now public domain: search and ye shall find. The project is 'company confidential' at your firm, but Google it and it's amazing what you find – all of which will help your case, of course.

'The greatest danger is not that we aim too high and miss it but that we aim too low and reach it.'
MICHELANGELO

Defining idea...

How did it go?

Q **What's the point in reading about how to influence if I can't get what it is I really want? I just want what I want.**

A *Ninety-nine per cent of the time, influencing is a two-way thing. Few of us have 100% control over another person unless we are holding a gun to their head. So, we have to be careful when we starkly say 'we want what we want, full stop'. Flexibility creates solutions. Say you really want them to give you a company car-parking spot so you no longer get parking fines, but it just isn't going to happen. What about these two options: (1) they pay for a train season ticket; (2) they change your times to allow you to come in earlier so you can park in one of the very few on-street-parking slots? You are getting what you want, but in a slightly different way.*

Q **Okay, I can see that it would be helpful if I didn't refuse to budge, but isn't it a slippery slope to losing out? How flexible should I be?**

A *How long is a piece of string? Be as flexible as you wish to be. It is probably best to be as flexible as you need to be, though; otherwise you may go home empty-handed. It is, of course, easier to get all of what you want if you are in a strong position: if you are one of the few coders in the country who can do that level of software architecture, you can probably stick out for that salary. If your landlord finds it very difficult to find tenants for such a small flat in such an area, you can probably hold out for the concessions you want. One tip, though. You need to live with these people, so bear in mind that whenever you influence, it's not just about 'stuff', it's about your future relationships with them, too.*

15
Stick to your main point

Don't ask for too many things all at once. It's confusing to the other person and actually it may well end up confusing you. Keep it simple.

One thing tends to be easy. Easy tends to be understood. Anything understood is likely to be acted upon. That allows you to influence.

'... and while we're discussing why you've not done your homework, I had a call from your history teacher and she says you haven't done your coursework submission. Which reminds me: why do I always have to ask you for the clothes that need washing? I've given up on getting you to do your own laundry, but you could at least help me a bit here. And we need to talk about you and girls and parties especially early in the week ... and what's happening with your allowance by the way ...?'

Are you confused? Yes – and I bet this teenager is, too!

'... so, we need to talk about performance and why it's not where we would like it to be. Also I need to discuss the new pension plan arrangements and how we've

Here's an idea for you...

Have you heard of the Pareto principle, or the 20/80 principle? Thought so. In essence, it means 80% of the results come from 20% of the effort. It's brilliant for focusing our efforts when influencing. For instance, if your landlord is a real rogue and everything needs fixing, just work on the rent reduction as that will have the biggest impact; if your teenage daughter is being very difficult at the moment, just work on getting regular one-to-one discussions with her as that will have the biggest impact; if you'd like to earn money from writing, just work on getting what you feel is your 'best' article submitted to as many magazines as possible.

changed expense claims. Plus I expect you will have a few points you wish to raise ... and if we can get that all done in about an hour that would be great ... Sorry, let me just answer my phone ...'

Is this going to be a good discussion with your employee? No, it's not!

'... children would be nice and, of course, that would be another reason for living in the country, and probably we could get more for our money and so we'd have a room for my mum so when she's staying she wouldn't annoy you so much ...'

You see – and you know this deep down – we humans are simply not good at multitasking. We cannot handle too many points at a time. So, leave multitasking to your laptop and stick to the point – especially when trying to influence somebody.

Good influencing is:
- A clear main point – e.g. rent reduction. (Ask: what's the one thing I want?)
- Clarity at all times – e.g. a rent reduction of 5%. (Ask: if I had to measure what I wanted, how would I do that?)

- One point at a time – e.g. let's talk rent reduction, then we can talk about maintenance. (Ask: does that point lead to that point?)
- Putting it in writing – e.g. to summarise our meeting ....

Poor influencing is:
- Vagueness
- Confusion
- A shifting goal
- Over-reliance on verbal conversations (I don't remember you saying that ...).

So, how do we get clear on what we want? Here are three good ways of doing that.

Method 1 (useful if you are on your own): Write it out. Writing forces us to clarify what we mean. Then read it back: check for assumptions, multiple requests or simple confusions.

Method 2 (useful if there is someone who can help you): 'Explain' to another person what you want. See if they can understand it. Ask them to pick holes in your points. Get them to be tough with you.

Method 3 (useful with high-risk influencing, such as negotiating the sale of your business): Find someone who has experience and (paying them if necessary) get an hour or so with them to check your points. Again, get them to be tough with you.

'The main thing is to make the main thing the main thing.'
STEPHEN COVEY, business author

Defining idea...

59

Q   **But surely using the Pareto idea means you have to leave things out, doesn't it?**

A   Yes. The Pareto approach does mean that you do not exhaustively cover everything but that means you avoid exhaustion. And when you avoid exhaustion, you are more likely to achieve a result. If you try to influence everyone in that committee meeting about everything, you may well fail. Instead, take the big message to the main people. Coupled with this is the important point that the human brain can only take on so many points. When attempting to have it our way we are always balancing 'completeness' versus 'simplicity'. Pareto should be a healthy compromise between the two.

Q   **But some influencing is very complicated – this leads to this, which leads to that, and so on. What should I do if I can't stick to one central point?**

A   Pareto is a principle not a rule. It's helpful, but cannot be used all of the time. If you are doing some formal influencing – say with the bank manager about extending your loans – then there will be interconnections and implications. A top tip here is to map things out on a pad or, preferably, a white-board that you and the bank manager can both see clearly. That way, you can study the complicated picture while at the same time keeping the key issues in mind.

16

Have emotions, but don't be emotional

We all have emotions, of course; that's what makes us human. But you must manage those emotions or they might spoil your argumentation.

You may think good influencing is all about being totally logical. Wrong. There is always a place for emotions so long as you keep them under control. Read on and discover how.

You will always have an emotional response. The fact that your HR department has said 'no more free coffee' is okay, you suppose, but you're really annoyed about the end to the subsidy for gym membership. And the reason it annoys you is that you *know* that with the company's buying power they could help you (and many others) get a reduced subscription. You need to influence their decision and you are angry.

The fact that your girlfriend lent some of your CDs to one of her friends without asking wasn't *so* bad, but you're *livid* that now, after two months, she won't help you get them back. Sure, the tracks are on your MP3 player, but that's not the point, is it? You need to influence and you're livid.

If you're feeling angry/upset/furious and it's about a situation you want to change, then try these tips. *Walk:* **walking is a great way to harness the anger and/or frustration, and as you walk, think about what you are going to say.** *Newspaper:* **take the newspaper, roll it up into a long cylinder and bash it hard along the edge of a table or the back of a chair – notice how much better you feel.** *Write:* **put pen to paper or fingers to keyboards and as you write you will soon feel a whole lot better.** *Gym:* **that running machine or those free weights will soon get you refocused.**

You've just been shunted on the slip road down to the motorway. Here you go: insurance exchange time. But how is it going to go: amicably (it might as well, mightn't it?) or with hostility, which will spoil your day and maybe lessen your chances of a rapid solution?

These emotions are normal, because you are normal. But – and it's an important but – we need to channel that emotion into being helpful, not detrimental. With practice, we can turn that emotion into something that enables us to do an even better job rather than something that causes us to explode and 'lose it all'.

The way we do this is through some kind of physical activity with our body because that's where the anger has 'ended up'. It started mentally and has produced a range of powerful chemicals – such as adrenalin – that need to be used or dissipated. 'Using' might mean punching someone or swearing and using sarcasm, which is, of course, generally not helpful in mature adult-to-adult influencing. These reactions are remnants from our evolutionary past.

Dissipating means using the adrenalin 'rush' in a more positive way. The number one and most important and beneficial aspect of dissipation is that of causing action. If you are angry you want to do something. And that's great. You are so angry, you are going to get those CDs back! You are so angry with HR's silly decision, you are going to do something about it!

What's particularly interesting is because you are angry and you manage that anger to take action you tend to get change, get a result, get success and that makes you feel better, which finally dissipates the anger as new chemicals fill your body.

So, to summarise:

- Something happens and you are not happy about it: something needs influencing.

- You become angry: adrenalin flows. It could result in 'caveman' behaviour, but you are channelling it so that it becomes 'action' behaviour. The action causes you to influence particularly well.

- You end up successful and that releases 'feel-good' chemicals.

- That rewards the excellent behaviours you adopted and you become better overall at influencing.

'Anyone can become angry – that is easy. But to be angry with the right person, to the right degree, at the right time, for the right purpose, and in the right way – that is not easy.'
ARISTOTLE

Defining idea...

Q   **Should I do this whenever I am angry?**

A   *Yes. It's always a good strategy when trying to influence to be aware of our emotions and what we will say next; to be a good listener; to be sensitive. We lose all of these fine, soft skills when we become angry. So, walk, write, thrash a newspaper – whatever it takes. Remember, though, it's clearly not wrong to be angry. In many ways that anger can give us the 'kick' we need to take action. It's what we do with that anger that's so important.*

Q   **Isn't it ever appropriate to just be emotional and let rip?**

A   *Let's be clear: we are always emotional. That's what it is to be human. What we have been talking about is channelling that emotion to use it to help our influencing rather than weakening our argumentation. If you get plain old-fashioned angry – ranting and shouting etc. – it's not effective. By definition, you are out of control and therefore may well say things you'll regret. Of course, if it does happen, the person who is on the receiving end will know you're serious and maybe it'll be just the thing to show that you have simply had enough. But, be careful: you can probably only do it once. You have been warned!*

17

Have fun

Rarely does it need to be all seriousness. If you have a laugh along the way and smile a bit more, you'll keep it relaxed, you'll curb defensiveness and you'll influence better.

The worst types of influencing discussions are the ones that polarise very rapidly. 'Yes, you did.' 'No, I didn't.' 'You did!' 'I didn't!' 'Did!' 'Didn't!' You're going nowhere.

It is essential when we are trying to influence that we keep the conversation going; that we maintain a flow. How can we do this? A brilliant way is through humour – or, perhaps, 'light heartedness' would be the better term. You'll have it your way more quickly and more easily. Consider this story:

Paul, a scientist, was working at home one day on some complex algorithms. He'd been hunched over a computer for hours; it was time for a walk. He was very fortunate that he lived in the country and he headed out to the beautiful rolling hills. Already as he paced he was feeling better.

Here's an idea for you... **Before an important bit of influencing, especially one about which you feel a little 'intense', read or watch something funny. Humour is often very individual, but you'll have something that works for you. It doesn't need to be 'laugh out loud', just something that turns your overly furrowed brow into a face that looks more receptive!**

As he rounded a bend, he was amazed to see the hillside totally covered with grazing sheep – hundreds and hundreds of them, as far as the eye could see. And then he noticed the shepherd and wandered over to chat to him.

Paul: Wonderful job, I imagine, being a shepherd.

Shepherd: Oh yes, I'm very lucky. Plenty of fresh air!

Paul: So you enjoy it?

Shepherd: Yes – been in the family for generations. What do you do?

Paul: Oh, I'm a scientist. I have a question. I hate mowing my lawn and have often wondered, if I got a sheep, would that do the job for me?

Shepherd: Well, it would certainly keep the grass down. You'd not get the neat stripes, of course!

Paul: Hmm, if I could tell you how many sheep you have on these hills, exactly, would you give me one of your sheep?

Shepherd: Well, I don't give them away you know; they're worth a lot. But if you could do that, I'd be so impressed that I would give you one.

Paul: Okay – 731 sheep.

Shepherd: That's amazing! I don't know how you did that, but help yourself to an animal.

Paul: Thanks.

Paul wandered down the track back to the valley where he lived. After a few minutes, the shepherd knocked on his door.

Shepherd: If I could tell you what kind of scientist you are, could I have my animal back?

Paul: Sure. I don't think you'll ever guess!

Shepherd: You are a theoretician.

Paul: How did you know that?

Shepherd: The animal you have taken is my dog!

See, a bit of fun makes you feel better. Feeling better helps oil the wheels of influencing, in particular the ability to be more flexible. Develop a light-hearted approach by:

'Stupid people, who do not know how to laugh, are always pompous and self-conceited; that is, ungentle, uncharitable, unchristian.'
WILLIAM MAKEPEACE THACKERAY

Defining idea...

67

- Respecting the other person's views and listening to them properly, with positive body language. Don't judge too quickly – ask for clarification before dismissing anybody's ideas.

- Using welcoming and friendly language. Thank people for their contributions – they'll work so much better when appreciated.

- Planning, so that all of your points are collected together and easy to understand. Work on what's most important, not necessarily everything on your mind.

- Taking breaks. If any stress is building, it will be relieved by some time out.

When you have a bit of fun, when you are light hearted, you remove pressure, you keep people open, all of which are tremendously important when influencing. Taking it all too seriously will cause the influencing to move into an argument all too quickly.

Q **Can't it be dangerous using humour? Some people might think you're not fully committed or not taking things seriously.**

How did it go?

A *Yes, certainly, humour needs to be used with care. But humour does not necessarily mean laugh-out-loud gags; it's more a sense of light heartedness. For example: in a discussion with your girlfriend about keeping the flat clean, just stop and give her a hug; in a discussion with your boss about pay scales, pause and mention 'this is a great company and I do want to keep working for it, you know!'; in a discussion with your supplier about discount rates, remind them of how heated they got in the very first negotiation you had five years ago and how you both laugh about it now. It's that kind of thing ...*

Q **I'm just a serious person; people often say that to me. What can I do if I'm supposed to lighten up?**

A *You don't need to become a stand-up comic. Two tips though: smile a bit more; it'll help tremendously. And don't feel you have to be absolutely right or complete in your arguments. There is absolutely no reason at all why you can't use light heartedness in helping you to 'have it your way' – you simply need to find your style. Try reading and watching more 'humorous' material to get you thinking that way more often.*

18

Que? Speak their language

However brilliant your argument, if nobody understands it you might as well give up and go home. You won't get anybody on board without a compelling case.

When we need to influence somebody to have it our way, we must work hard not only to make our point unarguable but also to ensure the other person can understand easily why it is important.

Have you ever been on a foreign holiday – say in Italy – and observed a tourist aiming to confront a problem – say about a restaurant bill – and they are doing it by shouting … in English! It's not going to work, is it? But sometimes we do the same even when we are all working in English: we simply are not talking 'their language'.

Just as English-to-French or Italian-to-Mandarin is not going to work without a translator on the scene, there's little chance of you successfully influencing if you're ranting about child-care difficulties from a single mother's perspective at a male head teacher who has never experienced anything but a traditional family background. Face it: it's just not going to work.

Here's an idea for you...

Think about the next influencing situation you've got coming up and pre-empt the communication breakdown by planning your ripostes. Take a sheet of paper and draw a line vertically down the middle. This, believe it or not, is going to be your vocabulary book. On the left-hand side, jot down some phrases you know are going to come up in that discussion. On the right-hand side, write down the translation. For example with your teenage daughter: she says 'you don't understand me', your translation 'I understand you only too well'. With the bank manager: he says 'it's not a viable business proposition', your translation 'it sounds pretty good but as you don't have security ...'

Ranting at your daughter about what it was like when you were a teenager ... it's just not going to go anywhere. And whatever the bank manager says about how he 'understands what it's like to run a small business', he doesn't – not really. He's never had to get his own head around what it's like to run a business. So talking to him from your perspective just isn't going to work.

To influence someone, we must talk their language and use their kind of vocabulary. To the builder, ask 'Will you be done with the scaffolding by next Saturday?' rather than 'Are you going to pass the next milestone on my schedule on time?'. To your daughter say 'I'm sure we could be getting along better', rather than 'I think we have a relationship issue'. We must use relevant examples and language that makes sense.

We must respect other people's intelligence. And – here's a tough one – we must assume that, most of the time, people do what they think is perfectly sensible. Much of the time they are not necessarily trying to 'wind us up'. Our daughter just thinks we did things differently when we were younger and things aren't the same now. The builder feels he's done a good day's work and he can't do much more. And so it goes on.

So, talking 'their' language is about communicating in ways that they can understand, make sense and are relevant. For example, compare these two approaches (a team leader trying to influence shop-floor staff to be more customer-focused):

1. Look, we've simply got to get the customer service metrics up. They're around 85% at the moment; it is simply not good enough because New World of Work marketing requires a threshold of at least 90%. To be honest some of you are in real danger of being 'let go' if we don't sort this out.

2. Okay, so, everyone got some tea or coffee? Great. Now before the shop opens I want to go right back to some basics about working with our customers. Yes, yes, I know we talk about it a lot but it is the difference that makes all the difference. Can anyone give me some example of great service they have received when out shopping? … That's what I mean …

'Language is not only an instrument of communication, or even of knowledge, but also an instrument of power. One seeks not only to be understood but also to be believed, obeyed, respected, distinguished.'
PIERRE BOURDIEU, French sociologist

Defining idea…

You see how it works: drop the jargon, drop the ego and talk real.

How did
it go?

Q **But what about if that's part – if not all – of the problem and I simply can't speak the right language? This business I work in is just about making as much money as possible. I was led to believe differently at my interview. We screw the customers left, right and centre. And however I try and tackle it, it just doesn't seem to work. Care, compassion, bigger picture humanity contribution 'give back' – these are simply not words that people understand in this business. I'm sick of it and I want to leave.**

A *If the difficulties of influencing are part of a bigger picture, such as if your own heart is not really in the job or you feel your employers are not supporting your efforts to engage with your customers, then moving on is probably the only option. Business is about money, though, and we do often need to be pragmatic, but if you can't influence by speaking the language of your company or the customers, feel happy to jump ship.*

Q **I'm going to be difficult for a moment: why shouldn't *they* make an effort to speak *my* language.**

A *If they are smart, they will do, so make sure you keep an eye out for it. But remember one thing: not everyone is as smart as you! And isn't it nice being 'multilingual': that's effectively what you are. People will envy your ability to relate to so many different groups; from mothers at the toddler group to builders on site, to the regional bank manager to the receptionist. That's a real skill you've got. Plus – just as when you are abroad and you make an effort in the local language – once you make an effort, those around you will, too.*

19

WIIFM? (What's in it for me?)

Most people will do anything so long as you give them a 'why' that's big enough. And that's what great influencing is about: giving a really big why.

To come up with incentives that ensure you will have it your way, you need to get into other people's heads and understand what motivates them.

Of course your boss doesn't want to give you a salary increase: that increase has got to come from somewhere else. And if you get an increase, the danger is everybody else will want one.

Of course your son doesn't want to stay in revising for his exams. Nobody else is doing it yet and consequently he is going to look very un-cool if he does so.

So, your challenge when influencing is to identify a big enough 'why'. Why your boss should give you that increase; why your son should stay in. Why she should go out with you. Why he should move out again. Why the gas board should give you a refund. Why the family holiday should be Spain and not Devon this year. What we

Here's an idea for you... **Think of the whys that will get the others to go along with you in your current influencing situation. Then practise 'chaining' them – just keeping using another 'and'. For example, the reason the church will allow us to use their fete area is: Many of us attend the church *and* ... We are offering to make a large donation to church funds *and* ... We will repair one of the fences in the field free of charge *and* ... We will write a nice article about how helpful the vicar has been.**

are searching for is an answer to the question, 'What's in it for me?' – and that answer needs to be: 'Plenty!'

That's how to find a great why. We think about what's in it for them, from their perspective: the winning answer to 'WIIFM?'. Here are some examples (and notice how we 'chain' the process).

Why should my boss give me an increase? What's in it for him? He gets to keep me; that means he keeps my experience; that experience is getting more and more valuable; it's getting harder and harder to find such experience on the open market; he's actually saving a lot of money by giving me an increase.

Why should Joe stay in and do exam revision? What's in it for him? He gets to feel more confident with the material; he reduces stress and he increases his chances of success; he may be less cool now but he will be more cool later when he gets that job at the BBC he really wants because of the excellent qualifications he has.

Why should Tom's school allow him to do both music and design, which is a major clash on the timetable? Well, firstly, you will keep him at the school rather than transfer him to somewhere that can cope with this subject mix. But also, you'll ensure that an article appears in the local paper about the school's amazing flexibility.

Why should the builder give you a refund? After all, there's nothing in writing that says you asked him to use the cheaper tiles behind the cupboards. You don't threaten him with a solicitor's letter but say that you will continue to recommend him to all of your contacts in the area. Also, you can give him a nice bit of extra work rebuilding the garden wall, which you'd been thinking of leaving to someone else.

Remember the foundations of a good 'why' are often:

- Money: making more
- Time: having more
- Life: being less stressful
- Relationships: closer, more loving
- Business: quicker, easier
- People: better reputation, higher status.

Search for anything you can offer that focuses on these as a starting point.

'But after observation and analysis, when you find that anything agrees with reason and is conducive to the good and benefit of one and all, then accept it and live up to it.'
BUDDHA

Defining idea...

And one final point. In general, our answer to 'WIIFM?' should be positive, but sometimes – and with great care – it can be worth highlighting the negatives if the change is not made. If you don't do your revision you'll get poor results, which means you won't get to work at the BBC.

How did it go?

Q I'm not sure how to say this, but I can't see that there are any benefits for them! Where do I go from here?

A   *In which case you have a problem! To influence someone, we have to be able to motivate them to change and to motivate them to change we have to give them at least one good* why. *It's possible that you can't think of a good benefit for them at the moment. Give it time. Go back to the ideas above. Go on a walk. There is a reason and when you relax a bit, it will come to you.*

Q Should I remind them of the benefits to me?

A   *It depends on the kind of influencing you are doing. Broadly speaking, the closer, more intimate, more long-term, more straight-talking the influencing, then yes, remind them of the benefits to you. For instance, in the early weeks of a brand new relationship, ground rules are being set that could last for years to come and it will (hopefully!) be very much a two-way dialogue about the benefits to both of you. On the other hand, if you are simply influencing the supermarket to give you a refund on the broken barbecue you bought from them, simply stress how delighted you will be to tell all your friends how agreeable they were!*

20

No more toddler tears: theirs or ours

Influencing our young children is probably one of the toughest challenges. How do we do it effectively without creating long-lasting psychological scars? For them or us.

Your young children — you love them dearly, of course, but it's a battle royal to get them to do what you want and have it your way. Let's look at what you face.

You want them to tidy their room, brush their teeth, go to bed, eat up their food, be nice to granny, not use crayons on the walls, not eat worms. Just when you have sorted those ones out you need to influence them into not swearing or telling lies. And then it's important that they do their homework, learn their spellings, watch their diet, learn how to tie their shoelaces, not to mention saving some of their pocket money instead of spending it all on sweets.

Phew ... what a list! Every one of them is a minor influencing scenario.

Here's an idea for you...

It's called 'the sandwich'. Whenever you are influencing one of your children, start with good news, then handle the problem, and then end on good news. Thus: 'Zoë, your teacher said you're really doing some great drawings at the moment. I saw two of them today: they are lovely. Now, speaking of art, I really do want all paints cleared out of the kitchen before supper. Please will you do that for me? If you keep up this great work, I think granny will want to introduce you to watercolours.'

Yep, being a good parent is back-to-back and wall-to-wall influencing. And, to be honest, some of the tricks we use with adults – bribery, sulking, offering money, threatening to leave – are simply not great approaches with children. (Actually, they're not so great with adults either.)

So, what is the best approach? There are some remarkably easy, but also very powerful, rules that apply.

Rule 1: Be consistent
Rule 2: Be loving
Rule 3: Reward positive behaviour
Rule 4: Be clear; give detail
Rule 5: Be adult

Let's clarify each of these:

Rule 1: Be consistent. The world is, of course, rarely black and white; it is 'fuzzy' around the edges. That fact's a bit much for young children, so in general try to keep it as black and white or yes and no as you can for them. It'll help you have it your way if you are consistent. There are times for sweets (Saturday afternoon, perhaps) and times not for sweets (like between meals). Decide the rules and keep to them, and that's that.

Rule 2: Be loving. Whatever happens, your children need to know you always love them. After you have dealt with the water spilt all around their bedroom and how it mustn't happen again, give them a big hug and read a bedtime story as usual. Yes, you told them off; yes, they know not to do it again. But, yes, they also know that you love them.

Rule 3: Reward positive behaviour. This is about catching them doing things right and noticing good behaviours, like putting their plates in the dish-washer and tidying their bedrooms. Thank them. Yes, we know they ought to do it, but thank them anyway.

Rule 4: Be clear; give detail. What exactly does 'tidy up the playroom' mean? Put the toys in the boxes? But do the boxes have to go in the cupboard? And are they meant to vacuum the floor, too? Make sure that they know.

Rule 5: Be adult. Treat them as an adult and then, with luck, they will begin to behave like one. Use 'grown-up' explanations and language. Not, 'That was a stupid thing to do to your baby brother'; rather 'Your brother's much younger than you so he doesn't always behave as well as you – we have to give him a second chance'.

'**Acting is not life; my children are my life.**'
DENZEL WASHINGTON

Defining idea...

So, let's try it out. Young Tom is not eating well. He eats, but it's junk food. You want to influence him to eat more variety, in particular more fruit and vegetables. Let's try it by the rules.

1. Be consistent by always providing healthy food. Don't cheat and serve junk food at some meals – that would simply confuse him.

2. Be loving by ensuring meal times are a pleasure – chat, laugh and have fun.

3. Reward Tom's positive behaviour by making an extra fuss of him when he eats the vegetables – we all like to get extra attention.

4. Be clear about which foods are for growing and health and which are occasional 'treat' foods.

5. Be adult in demonstrating that you always eat healthy foods. Explain to Tom why some foods are healthy and others are not.

Q   **This is really hard. To be honest, I know I am being too soft on the children at times. But I see so little of them, how can I be tough with them?**

How did it go?

A   *You'll have probably heard people use terms such as quantity time and quality time. They are distracting terms. Think 'contact time' – when you are with your children, really be with them; not thinking about your e-mail, not talking into a mobile phone above their head. Once you are connecting with them you can afford to stay loving but occasionally be firm. Children actually like to know where the boundaries are.*

Q   **Should I sometimes just accept defeat? Like with cutting out junk food? At least they are eating something!**

A   *Yep, it is hard. Peer pressure, coupled with consumer pressure and on top of that the 'good advice' of family and friends can make it tough to influence your children. But, if it's important to you, it will happen if you stick at it. Just because 'they' let their children watch certificate 18 videos at age 12 does not mean you need to. Yes, there will be a battle, but it's worth winning. That's good influencing and good parenting.*

21
Young adults: where did your kids go?

Rational logic seems to go out of the window with young adults. You need to be cunning to influence them and to get the agreements to stick.

There's so much to discuss, so much to help them with: education, relationships, money, drinking, sex. If only they would listen, and stop thinking they know best all the time.

The challenge here lies with that second word: young *adults*. They do believe they are adults and they do believe they are right. Why? Two reasons. One is the healthy self-esteem that you have nurtured in them since they were a kid. You know: all those sessions at the park, the music lessons, the debates at the supper table – it has all come back to bite you. Also, society wants them to be adult. Cynically we could say society wants them to be consumers as soon as possible. Whatever the reason, it wants them to move from baby to toddler to child to adult as quickly as possible.

Here's an idea for you... **Start early. The earlier you start building a healthy relationship with your son and/or daughter, the easier you'll find it when they are teenagers. Work on this from the start. Read to them. Talk to them. Spend time (especially one-to-one) with them. Adapt as they change. Stay interested in what they find interesting and stay interesting. If you share a passion – rugby, riding – you're definitely in a good place.**

What's to be done? For starters, you need to get back to quality conversations, and we're not going to promise any quick fix on this. Given a bit of time, though, you can become a great influencer with this age group.

Resurrecting those quality conversations is a tough job but here's a suggestion: forget the conversation, create the *activity*, be it pub, pool, walking, shopping. Whatever: create the activity and the conversation will happen. The last thing a young adult wants is that serious, sit-down-at-the-table conversation – the one where they look bored, act bored and are bored; the one where they mumble yes, no, or maybe at appropriate time intervals.

Say you've found an activity they enjoy with you and the conversation has started to flow. Tip two is to be a listener and encourager rather than a teller and judger. A listener and an encourager spends time understanding his/her son's/daughter's perspective and then encouraging the best in that and building on it. A teller and judger delivers speeches and focuses on what's wrong. Compare the two styles.

Teller and judger: ... if you carry on like this you're going to end up failing your exams, and then what's going to happen? I'll tell you what's going to happen ... and no you're wrong ... very few people make it as rock stars, you know ... most end up without a job ... Okay, accountancy doesn't sound cool but ... after all, I wouldn't say I exactly enjoy my job but it's meant we could send you to a decent school ... and it would be nice to see a little more gratitude for that.

Listener and encourager: (In a conducive environment; in Starbucks after a bit of shopping; down the pool hall after a couple of games.) I was wondering: how's the exam preparation going? Yeah, I know it's one of the toughest things we have to do. It's good that you are at least aware it needs to be done. How can I help? No problem: I don't mind helping out with money for revision books. And shall I help you draw up a revision timetable?

Go where they want to go in the conversation, even if it is apparently nowhere, or they are initially monosyllabic. Remember young adults are going through huge physical changes. These cause tiredness (they really do need lots of sleep), emotional changes, lack of confidence, rebelliousness. They are also being heavily influenced by a consumer society. They are under pressure to get top exam results. If, with all that happening, they know you are on their side, the influencing channels will always stay open.

'The best substitute for
experience is being sixteen.'
RAYMOND DUNCAN, artist

Defining
idea...

87

Q **I think we go too far with understanding and listening. Aren't there some areas where the answer is just plain 'no' – zero tolerance if you like?**

A   *Absolutely right. The important thing is to decide what they are for your family. (What are your limit points on drugs, for example?) None of these are easy issues to resolve but they are certainly worth tackling. You cannot influence unless you know what the parameters are, and it's best to agree them before you need to refer to them! Plus, of course, it will be easier to have one or two no-go areas if, in general, you are willing to listen and discuss. Remember to be flexible and agree updates – a rule for when they are aged 12 probably needs to be updated when they reach 15.*

Q **What about the differences between boys and girls?**

A   *Yes, there are many differences and many of them are hugely significant – interests, emotional development, study skills, to name just a few. But probably the best thing is to not generalise with your own children; just use the skills we've been talking about above to discover what works and what doesn't work for your sons/daughters. Many boys – in general – are not as emotionally mature as girls of the same age. But maybe your son is very emotionally mature, even a bit of a poet. That needs encouraging, so show an interest. And your daughter happens to be quite mechanically minded and wants to get a holiday job working in a garage. Great. Just remind her how to deal with sexist men and then she'll have a great time.*

22

Men! How to influence your Martian

You love him – you really do – but he is such a pain at times. You need to learn how to be brilliant at influencing your boyfriend.

Because so much appears to be at stake, we sometimes do and say crazy things with the men we love, which can of course often have dire consequences later.

Women the world over will identify with these perennial sources of frustration. Why, oh why, does he ...

- Not make an effort with appearance when you go out?
- *Never* tidy up around the flat?
- Leave you to do all the food planning?
- Show no interest in the films you would like to see?
- Talk so much about other girls – especially the very pretty ones?
- Talk about you (often rudely) behind your back?
- Refuse to talk about marriage and children?
- Make cynical comments about the self-help books you read?

Here's an idea for you... **Identify some changes you want and the influencing you need to do – getting a longer term perspective on this relationship, what his real views on children are, etc. Then think how you could make progress. Bear in mind that the one thing that will work is talking. You need a decent conversation: one quality conversation and it could all be 'sorted'. So, when do you have your best conversations? When you are both relaxed; when you've got a bit of time; when there are no distractions such as football on TV? Choose that time. And don't try to 'sell' the idea of talking. Many men will see 'the need to talk' as 'psycho-babble'. Just get the conversation going by starting in their arena. Try it: you'll be amazed at how easily it works.**

As for the targets of these gripes, they no longer try to say anything to defend themselves or improve matters. As far as they're concerned, that's just an express train to argument time.

Actually, it's not so bad because you can view that list as a list of symptoms – and the majority of those symptoms can be boiled down to just one or two causes. It's a similar deal to having flu. You feel awful, your legs ache, your nose is running, you've got a sore throat, and a temperature. Those are the symptoms, but the root cause is the flu. What we need to find here is the root cause of what's getting to you: that's what we need to work on. So here it is, split into two points.

Point 1
Remember when you had 'the talk' – yes, the one about sex. Maybe it was at school, maybe with friends or maybe, horror of horrors, it was with your parents. It was useful in the end. But funnily enough, generally nobody gives you 'the talk' about relationships. Here it is.

Men and women are different – very different. You know that. That's what makes relationships such potential fun, but we do need to work with that difference rather than against it.

To be politically correct we spend a lot of time avoiding saying it, but the sexes do not conduct themselves in the same way. That doesn't stop us wanting and ensuring men and women get equal opportunity, equal support, etc. However, we will only get on well with each other if we recognise, respect and value that difference. And this is the key foundation that is essential to good influencing.

Here's the bottom line: your boyfriend is highly unlikely to think and respond like you and others of your sex. Ever!

Point 2
No change will happen unless you are communicating and respecting the differences between you. Communication will start if you can talk to your man about his interests and embrace the fact that he ticks differently. Yes, he does go on about cars a lot, but that's what interests him. So, try to show an interest in his interests and don't judge. Then, guess what: he'll start talking, and not just about cars. And then when you are talking you can introduce some of your own points.

'How can a woman be expected to be happy with a man who insists on treating her as if she were a perfectly normal human being?'
OSCAR WILDE

Defining idea...

91

How did it go?

Q   **Can our relationship ever work when we appear to differ on so many things: money, children ... the list goes on and on?**

A   *In many ways this is less about influencing and more about acceptance. We tend to fall in love with someone because of two main attractions. The most obvious one is physical attraction. We love their body, their eyes, their smile etc. That's 'attractiveness' as we all understand it. There is of course another aspect to attractiveness and that is 'mental attraction'. We're fairly organised; he's pretty spontaneous. That makes for a nice match. She's fairly arty whereas he's more practical: another nice match. Of course, though, under pressure, these mental attractions can get irritating. That's when we want to change or influence them. That's the danger sign! And that's probably when it's better to work on our acceptance first and foremost because there are some things about a person which are just about who they are. For instance, you can influence someone to pick up their dirty socks or to help you save to buy more for your flat, but you'll struggle if you're wanting to influence someone to 'like parties more'. That's about acceptance.*

Q   **It seems as if I'm making all the effort in this relationship. That's not fair, is it?**

A   *No it's not fair, but it is worth it as you will end up with an even better relationship, and there is almost nothing so exciting in life as a fantastic relationship that nearly always works well, is occasionally brilliant and always loving. Someone's got to start on that road so see yourself as that person. He'll get the idea eventually – he really will – and he'll love you even more for it. And, to be honest, if he doesn't, then maybe that's telling you he's not worth it and it's time to move on.*

23

Women! How to influence your Venusian

You do love her. But she seems to be trying to pin you down, take the fun out of your life and organise you. And you just don't want that yet.

One thing's certain: if you try influencing her as you do your mates, then you're in for real problems. You'll need finesse, style and a bit of emotional intelligence.

We all know that men and women are different and that's what puts the fun into relationships. The same difference can also be the cause of turmoil. To keep the relationship more fun than grief, we need to work with that difference rather than against it.

To influence her, try being the change you are seeking. If you want your girlfriend to be less controlling of you (why are you out so often with your mates?), be less controlling of her (clothes shopping is such a waste of time and money!). If you

Here's an idea for you... **Stop expecting your girlfriend to think and act like you. She never will. And you actually love her because she doesn't (think and act like you). Appreciate her for that. Use romance to tell her how much you do appreciate her. Plan a surprise for her today – why not book a meal at your favourite restaurant?**

want her to appreciate you for who you are (that's me: I'm brilliant with cars), be appreciative of her (wow: you are great with young children). The fastest way to influence her is less through what you say, but more through what you do.

Work on the relationship first, before you try and change anything else. Start doing more of the following:

- *Appreciating:* thank her more for making the flat look nice for visitors.
- *Hugging:* just hug, without it always leading to sex.
- *Listening:* take time to really understand what she's saying to you.
- *The small stuff*, like clearing up the debris of Sunday's breakfast in bed. Just do it.
- *Talking:* talk about feelings, about the future, about kids (if they are a possible part of your relationship) and your thoughts on schooling, on stay-at-home parenting.

Start doing less:

- *Judging:* why do you spend so much time shopping ...?
- *Cynicism:* that's a stupid book ...
- *Being a slob:* enough said.

You'll notice that the great thing about gentle influencing to get your relationship to work even better is that you don't need to change who you fundamentally are. (If you did have to, that would be very concerning.) You just need to do a few things which become perfectly easy and natural once done a few times.

A great relationship will mean that you can talk and you can talk about all kinds of things. A sign of an excellent personal relationship is one in which you can tackle difficult issues without it leading to a row; it's simply a topic of conversation.

Finally, stop worrying too much about 'logic' in your relationship. We, of course, do need logic with, say, our finances, but much of a great relationship is intangible and is not 'logical' in the strict 'if … then' kind of way. Allow your girlfriend to 'be'. Okay the car she has chosen to buy is not 'logical' in your terms because of its depreciation, but it is logical in her terms because it's small and fun.

'Women are meant to be loved, not to be understood.'
OSCAR WILDE

Defining idea...

How did it go?

Q It is possible that I'm simply not meant for a long-term relationship?

A *Perhaps, but it's more likely that you are. We do seem to be meant to have relationships, settle down, do stuff together etc. And when people say such things are dull or boring ('married life is dull'), it needn't be that way. Plenty of people show that it can be fantastic. The key is to decide that you will make it fantastic and forge the right long-term relationship. And how do you do that? By influencing what you can change (her rudeness about you spending a lot of time working on the car); accepting what you can't change (her lack of interest in cars); and invest in the relationship. If it's going to work you'll soon know.*

Q My girlfriend and I are like chalk and cheese – it's hard to imagine how we could be more different. Is that any basis for a lasting relationship?

A *This is all about a very important part of influencing: acceptance. How much can we change someone? A lot, certainly. But it is worth remembering that one of the reasons we fall in love with someone is that they offer us what we don't have ourselves. Opposites attract. So, trying to change someone too much may actually remove what made the relationship exist in the first place. If you're practical but she's a tad dippy, accept it because you won't change her. Accept that you'll enjoy helping her with practical things and she'll love you for it. Her spontaneity and energy will bring you out of yourself and you'll love her for that. However, if there are deep-rooted problems you really can't cope with, it's possibly about accepting you need a new relationship! Just remember that men are from Mars and women are from Venus.*

24
Wedded bliss

Been together for a long time? Yep, so long you've given up trying to change your other half. Well, that's not good for marital bliss.

Whatever we do as the years roll by, we shouldn't ever give up on him or her. Even after all this time, your husband/wife will still be easy to change — no, not for a new one!

Okay, there are some things that five years into your marriage you think: "Well, those things will never change now." And fifteen years in, you're thinking: "My fault – I shouldn't have accepted that in the first place." Think again because that's not so. A great marriage needs regular reinvention to keep it fresh and keeping on sorting out these kinds of issues does exactly that. Regular influencing is a great way to a healthy marriage.

The thing you've got to get out of your mind is that because it has been like this for a long time (and that's a relative term, of course: it doesn't really matter whether we are talking five, ten or fifteen years, or even longer), it's therefore fixed; it's stuck and you're doomed to put up with it. 'Long time' does *not* equal 'can't change'. Individuals change all the time. It's certain you've changed a lot over the past ten years, so why can't two people agree to make combined changes after all this time?

Here's an idea for you... **Fix a regular time every week or so for you both to get out of the house, get away from the kids, forget the e-mail and go somewhere where you can talk. Become adults again. Here are a few suggestions. A very relaxed meal in a nice local pub or restaurant. A walk in the park. A long coffee in a village café. A drive in the car and a sit in the car park overlooking the beach. You get the idea. If you wanted to, you could decide to do something different each time so that even planning your 'time out' becomes an enjoyable shared experience.**

They can.

Once we've got that mental block out of the way – i.e. change *is* possible – we need to think about what the best approach is.

Firstly, give a bit of thought to the change we really want: what do we really need to influence? Is it actually that he reads the newspaper at the breakfast table or that you never seem to talk any more? Is it actually that she's always out at various committee meetings or that it seems impossible to go out to a film or the theatre like you used to? So trace back the symptoms to the cause. Remember that many areas that require influencing revolve around money or sex (or both) but they are usually the symptom not the cause.

Here's the big idea: keep talking. Once you have identified the real issue (e.g. not planning for retirement) and not been distracted by symptoms (e.g. money arguments), then you need to talk it through and agree a plan. That can only happen if you have time to talk.

Whatever happens: keep talking. Never ever lose 'the thing' that keeps you talking. And don't just talk about the shopping or the kids' school reports: talk about you – fundamental stuff – in a non-rushed environment. We can't tell you how or when but we are betting you are intelligent enough to do that. So make it happen.

It's all about maintaining the emotional bank account. We all have one, just like our financial bank account. We have them with each other. The question is, are we making loads of deposits into the account (by being polite, being responsive, being helpful, being loyal) or are we making undue numbers of withdrawals (by being judgemental, rude, talking behind their backs)?

If we make plenty of deposits, the relationship can take the occasional withdrawals. But if it's been all withdrawals, the occasional deposit has little impact. Makes sense, doesn't it?

'[A] husband who can cook is not at all the same thing as a husband who can shop, prepare, and assemble ingredients, and clean up the mess after the great burst of creativity.'
MARY-JO FITZGERALD, *Marriage and the Male Animal*

Defining idea...

How did it go?

Q **As we've grown older we've both changed and it's actually made the differences between us seem even more prominent. Is that a sign that our marriage is heading for the rocks?**

A   *That almost suggests that you think you need to be the 'same' for the relationship to work. Actually, that could even make things worse. As we've said before, great relationships are built on differences – they add zest to our lives. If both of you can accept and work with these differences, then you have a healthy relationship. Importantly, though, this doesn't mean accepting everything and anything. She may be less time aware than you but always being late is not acceptable. He may be less interested in people than you but being rude to the neighbours is not acceptable. Remember, a great relationship is about asking for certain basics of communication, but then accepting differences until you might be able to bring your influence to bear.*

Q **My husband seems to have become more and more resistant to changing his ways these days and it feels like I'm making all the effort in this relationship. Should I just put up with it and hope for the best?**

A   *Keep plugging away with your influencing because it'll hopefully pay dividends in the long run. And remember that if your effort is shrouded in resentment, then it won't really work. If you do it with good grace, you should notice when your spouse begins to respond. It might take time, but the rewards will be worth it. And keep coming back to it. Keep trying different approaches. Sure, some relationships maybe are not going to work but most, with a bit of tender loving care, can be revitalised.*

25

Handling the boss

You may think the boss holds all the cards – after all, he can fire you. But that's not the whole story. You can influence your way to what you want.

You want to work part-time. They won't allow that: apparently, it's not company policy. Yes, you can, though. That's what this brilliant idea is about.

Once upon a time, the employer held all the power. Employees couldn't do anything for fear of losing their jobs. In the twenty-first century, that's no longer true. And this isn't to suggest in the cynical sense that so much of the legal system is now stacked against the employer that you can get away with murder. No, the situation has changed in a healthy and positive way for you.

Read this carefully and believe it: there are simply not enough great employees around. Think about it: the last bank you went into – what were the staff like? How about the restaurant where you ate last week, or your daughter's school? What are the people like there? Quite.

Here's an idea for you...

We know that great employees get what they want so analyse what makes a great employee. It's someone who has a 'can do' approach (*what can we do to get this policy to work?*), someone who is brilliant at the basics such as time management (*arrives at meetings on time*), someone who is customer service focused (*smiles and empathises when dealing with people*), someone who builds rather than destroys ('*it would have been good to have had more notice, but we didn't, so what can we do instead?*'). You're good at all of those, aren't you? Imagine what would happen if you became great at them. As you now realise, it's only one decision away.

There really is a shortage of excellent people for employers to choose from. So that's where we will start. Delay the influencing you need to do to get the change you want and start to shine like a great employee. Here's the deal: if you're a great employee, you cannot be replaced (or at least it is very hard to do so). That means you will be listened to and it means you have a good chance of getting what you want: you have become a fantastic influencer. Clever, huh?

No sane employer gets rid of great employees. Hence, great employees are good influencers. Start your influencing career by deciding to be excellent; deciding to be great.

But perhaps you think, 'Why should I? I am not paid enough to be excellent.' That's partly the point. Or maybe you think you will be excellent when you get the team leader's position. This is the trick most people miss: just be excellent for yourself. Nobody can take it away from you and, when you are, people want you. That's when you get listened to and you have your say.

If you're thinking you shouldn't have to raise your standards and you should simply have the right to go part-time, then you're not going to get very far with your ambition. It's the wrong mindset. If instead you decide to begin to enjoy getting better at the work and consequently do a great job, you will be recognised and you will start to get more of what you want: the corner office, then the promotion. And all without consciously influencing. It's a self-fulfilling prophecy.

Once you're an excellent employee, you'll have the boss's ear and that's when you can go for the jugular. Make sure you do it professionally, though. For instance:

■ get hard data for the changes you want (e.g. current salary ranges for your job)

■ book proper time for proper discussion and make sure you're fully prepared (e.g. to explain how the more flexible hours will help your child-care arrangements but won't alter your effectiveness)

■ build a relationship that fosters adult-to-adult conversation (i.e. don't allow yourself to be bullied)

■ respect the challenges your boss has, so fight the important battles.

Defining
idea...

'It is one of the strange ironies of this strange life [that] those who work the hardest, who subject themselves to the strictest discipline, who give up certain pleasurable things in order to achieve a goal, are the happiest people.'
BRUTUS HAMILTON, US athlete

Q **So, can you summarise what to do if I want a pay rise for example?**

A *We influence our employer by being so good that they want to listen to what we have to say; they want to keep us happy. We get to that point by raising our standards. We influence our employer by our behaviour and we influence them by who we are rather than just what we do. We become great at our job. We don't wait until we have got the pay rise, we act as if we have got it already. And after a couple of months of that, we set up the meeting at which we argue our case why we want an increase in salary. Support your argument with hard facts about how you're taking on more responsibility and the sort of salary you could get if you moved to another company.*

Q **But what if – and I'm being very honest here – I am not that great and there's no scope for me even to try to appear to be excellent?**

A *So, you are in the kitchen staff in a large comprehensive school and you are thinking, 'Well, it's just a job and there's not a lot to it apart from just turning up. He must be talking about people with jobs such as being a lawyer or even one of the teachers here ...'. No: think again! You do turn up, don't you? And you turn up on time. Just starting at that point makes you a better employee than many, so don't underestimate your own talent and offering. You already have a higher standard than many through great punctuality. Now look at other ways to raise that standard. For instance, become a better team player. Don't be so cynical. There's so much you can work on.*

26

Influencing the bank

Don't even mention my bank – head, meet brick wall! We will, because we are going to show you how to get exactly what you want from them.

Banks! Don't you just hate them? Most of us do — unreasonable charges, slow responses, constantly selling us stuff we don't want, arrogant, no personal touch.

We get introduced to our 'small business adviser' who, we're told, will look after us for at least the next twelve months. We ring up two weeks later and he has moved on. That's really not on. We are sort of vulnerable, because most of us need help with our finances every so often, even if it's just a mortgage and the occasional overdraft. So, how do we influence our banks – or, of course, any financial institution or big organisation that doesn't seem to be helping us as they should?

We play the game. And what does that mean? We work as they work. Let's be honest, there's one element of this you may not like to hear, so we'd better get it over and done with straight away. Actually it's best expressed in this comment made to a customer by a London bank: 'Mr Smith (name changed to protect, of course), we [the bank] would like to go back to the more usual arrangement where

Here's an idea for you...

Keep a special file for all of your dealings with the bank. If they are a typical bank, they will make mistakes; if you are human, you will forget things. Keep everything and put everything in writing; check everything. In the file, build up a structure-chart of the bank: who is your manager and who is their manager? Get e-mail addresses; don't allow them to be a large unfamiliar organisation. Get close and get what you want.

you bank with us rather than the other way around.' Okay, it's an old gag, but it gives us something to think about.

Here are some things to bear in mind about banks – or any major organisation – before we start ranting and raving at them:

1. Banks are in the business of managing and making money, not giving it away. Traditional high-street banks – which most of us deal with – are not in the business of risk. That's why they are constantly after security.

2. There are rules. Those rules are clearer than ever (e.g. when and what you will be charged for an overdraft). If we break these rules we will be punished and the simplest punishment is a charge.

3. Nobody likes being ignored, so if you do ignore communications, like notice about breaking an overdraft limit, then you will be punished even more.

It probably does seem unfairly biased to the bank, but that's the score. If we are going to be great at influencing, we must break this chain of thought which just says 'all banks are b*st*rds'. To influence your bank, you've got to do what most people don't do:

- *Be well-behaved.* Find out what you are able to do with the account you have and do not break the rules. Friends can be flexible. Banks cannot be. If your account does not do what you need, ring up the bank and make an appointment to see how you can get what you want.

- *Keep records.* Keep your statements and check them. If you have a meeting, ask for an e-mail address and put your conversation in writing and ask for the e-mail to be confirmed. Leave nothing to a verbal agreement – e-mail is quick and easy.

- *Point out mistakes quickly.* Provide the evidence and ask for mistakes to be rectified immediately.

- *Be assertive; don't get aggressive.* The person you are speaking to only has a certain level of authority. If they can't help you, ask to speak to the person who does have that authority. If you are blocked, put it in writing. All written correspondence has to be answered.

- *Be polite and persistent.*

- *Do stick with one bank.* Build up a track record and keep your files up to date. Sadly, though, you must accept that the days of developing a long-standing relationship with one manager are long gone.

Banks love people who are willing to work to their rules and who understand that the bank is not a charity. Once you can do that, you can start getting what you want.

'One rule which woe betides the banker who fails to heed it ... Never lend any money to anybody unless they don't need it.'
OGDEN NASH

Defining idea...

How did
it go?

Q **I really am in a financial mess. What's the best way to make a start on getting a handle on my money problems?**

A *If your finances are genuinely a total mess, then the bank can only help you to a limited extent. Talk to them honestly. Ask them how they can help. Remember, for instance, that they actually don't want to repossess your home; it's a lot of hassle and very unpleasant. So, be frank with them and tell them sooner rather than later. They will be able to introduce you to other agencies who can also help. Don't start taking out other loans; it'll be a slippery slope.*

Q **If I'm not happy with the service I'm getting at the moment, should I switch my account to another bank?**

A *Probably not. Despite what they say in their adverts, banks are all much the same. So, if your bank has an account structure you like and if the branch is handy (it's useful to get those face-to-face meetings every so often), then stick with them and build a relationship. Keep good records as evidence of their mistakes/agreements and your good practices. However, don't feel you need to do everything with one bank – just because your mortgage is with them doesn't mean your car loan has to be. And, as always, shop around, if only so that it gives you more negotiating power with your current bank.*

27
Influencing mum and dad

Good old mum and dad. They still want you to get a sensible job. And they still wonder what you see in your girl/boyfriend. You don't need to put up with it.

You love them, of course; but they drive you mad. Don't they know that you are 35 not 3.5? How do you influence them without hurting their feelings?

What a quandary. Sometimes you think that the more you try and be a good son/daughter, the more they interfere. But 'disconnecting' isn't fun either: family feuds are good for nobody. What's the problem? The problem really is that our rates of development are totally different. Just when we were taking off in our growth, both physical and mental, they were slowing down. So we see them as the same, and broadly they are. They see us still as children, but we're certainly not.

So, influencing our parents is really about getting them to see us in a different light; to make them take the huge leap from seeing us as a child to recognising us as an adult. And not just an adult, but as an adult who wants to make his/her own decisions, too, and who is happy to make his/her own mistakes.

Yes, we all live such busy lives, but it's vital to find quality time to spend with your parents. Plan it out. Then get into the habit of talking and talking. Don't follow them and start being judgemental. Encourage them to listen to you (by listening to them). Be interested, be curious and be interesting. It allows a connection to be made. Notice how out of those conversations some improvements come about. Having more time allows you to explain some things (well, actually, we see the children's education a little differently) and to be firm (no, I'm sorry I don't agree on that one). You'll be amazed at how the relationship begins to shift.

Until we bring about this image shift in their minds we will not get the one-to-one, adult-to-adult relationship, which is central to a healthy ability to influence our parents' thinking.

What's also true is that the earlier we do this, the easier it will be because as our parents get older there is a tendency for their thinking to get a little more fixed and perhaps a little less flexible.

How do we do it? We need to do what we often want to avoid; we need to invest some time with our parents. Of course, they are driving us mad, so we cut short the phone call. We storm off into the garden for a break from their lecturing or comments. We shorten the weekend visits. We go through the routine in conversations. And guess what? It just seems to get worse.

To influence our parents, we have to build an adult-to-adult relationship with them. For that to happen they have got to re-learn who we are. And for that to happen we have got to slow down and spend some time – some so-called quality time – talking to them, which will eventually generate quality conversations.

Because, at the moment, you are in the fast lane being very quick, it's causing the development of your influence to be slow. What we are going to do is slow down a bit and that will allow us to be quicker in achieving our influencing goals. It honestly *is* going to make things easier in the long term.

What you should be looking for are opportunities that create easy routes to conversations that can be extended and allow the relationship to be renewed. For instance, have a cooking day with your mum if she enjoys chatting in the kitchen. Have a few hours helping dad in his workshop if that's his passion. These one-to-one situations are a great start because it's so much easier to manage the conversation that way. Then you can move on to more involved conversations over family meals.

Defining idea...

'**The more boring a child is, the more the parents, when showing off the child, receive adulation for being good parents – because they have a tame child-creature in their house.**'
FRANK ZAPPA, interview in *Mojo* (1993)

How did it go?

Q **My relationship with my parents isn't healthy. They're getting older and less and less flexible. I dread having to talk to them about anything serious. I can't remember the last time I successfully influenced them on anything and yet there is so much that needs to be done to make their lives easier – and ours, too. What can I do?**

A *It's hard when you've reached a position like this and it can so easily creep up on any of us. The good news is that the basic principle we've explored in this idea – be slow in order to be quick later – does work no matter how awkward the relationship. The bad news is that it may take a little longer so you'll need to be extra tenacious and don't allow your impatience to show. Finally, remember that sometimes as parents get much older they may well get a little eccentric in some of their views and actions. Be prepared to do some accepting as well as influencing.*

Q **Any thoughts on how to influence expectations at those emotional hot-spots such as Christmas etc.?**

A *Yes! Start early – a change to the Christmas ritual is much more easily discussed at Easter rather than the first week of December. Avoid rituals – however much fun something is, be careful about regular events. Before you know where you are, you'll be getting, 'but we always go to CenterParcs the first week of the summer holidays'. Be honest – it can cause one painful conversation, but better that than sixteen awful Christmases. Give and take; be fair – if you have insisted that you want a quiet, intimate family Christmas, when will all the present swapping occur?*

28

Love thy neighbour

That bloody lawnmower at 7.00 on a Sunday morning is doing your head in. You need to learn how to reach positive agreements with the neighbours.

That overhanging tree is a pain and it's only going to become more of a nuisance. How do we influence the neighbours yet avoid falling out with them?

Why do neighbours do stuff like this: Allow their pets to foul our lawn and dig up our flower-beds? Shout so much? Cook curries at 8.00 in the morning? Throw bottles so loudly into the recycling bin? Slam the car doors loudly after returning from early Sunday service? Have a clapped-out, rusting motorcycle in the front garden? Have barbecues that go on long into the night on summer evenings – with that choice of music? And then they ignore you when you bump into them in the supermarket. Because they are neighbours, that's why.

So, how do we influence them? By bridge-building, not by ditch-digging. With hindsight, the Cold War seems like an utterly crazy time: if we were Russian, we thought capitalism was evil and we were about to be bombed to destruction; if we were living in the West, we thought communism was evil and we were about to be

Here's an idea for you... **Whether or not you have a problem with your neighbours, as soon as you move into a new house and/or a new area, do something, anything, that allows you to do some bridge-building. Get to know your immediate neighbours as quickly as possible, before any problems arise. Sometimes, it's very easy because you both have young children and you go to the same mother and toddler group or you drink at the same local. But sometimes a bit more effort needs to be made. Don't be lazy, it'll be worth it.**

bombed to destruction. And then eventually when it came down to it we were all the same.

It's the same with our neighbours: they're probably not so different to you; it's just you haven't really got to know them yet. You've got to bring down your Berlin Wall, metaphorically, of course. Or, if you can't pull down the wall, then go round. And that's what bridge-building is about.

It'll probably take time, but that's fine. Of course, they won't be just like you, but most people are basically okay. If you keep being nice (and it's no real loss to you, is it?), they'll end up being nice to you. They can't really keep up any nastiness!

Here's the ditch-digging conversation:

You: I'm not very happy about the tree overhanging our garden.
Them: Well, it's not far over and it's not doing any real harm.
You: That's not the point.
Them: What is the point then?
You: It's my garden and I don't want anything overhanging my property.
Them: You're being childish.
You: No I'm not; how would you like it?

Them: It wouldn't bother me.

You: Of course it would. I'm calling the police.

Them: You're daft – as if they'd be interested!

You: This has now become a criminal issue!

It's just not going to work, is it? Here's the bridge-building conversation:

Stage 1: During the week

You: Morning: we were thinking of having a barbecue. Fancy coming over on Saturday?

Them: Great. Jane and I were just saying we should do something together.

Stage 2: At the barbecue (after a steak, some sausages and three cans of beer)

You: By the way, I was wondering if we could work out something about the tree?

Them: In what way?

You: Well, it's overhanging. I'm certainly not worried about the tree itself, it's just that the overhang's keeping one of the few nice sunny spots we've got in the shade for most of the day.

Them: Well, feel free to cut it off then. Doesn't really bother me what happens over your side of the boundary.

You: You sure?

Them: Of course.

That's more like it!

Defining idea...

'**There are many who dare not kill themselves for fear of what the neighbours will say.**'
CYRIL CONNOLLY, English critic and novelist

One more time, here's a ditch-digging conversation:

You: Your son plays his drums too loud in the evenings.

Them: Well, you can't play drums quietly, can you?

You: He could play them another time.

Them: He's at college during the day. Anyway, why are you complaining?

You: Well our daughter needs to sleep after nine.

Them: He's not that loud.

You: Yes he is. And at ten at night.

Them: Well, he's going to be in a band, so he's got to practise.

You: So, you won't do anything about it?

Them: Can't really.

You: In that case, I'm going to contact the Environment Agency about the noise.

Again, it's just not going to work, is it? Here's the bridge-building conversation:

You: Hey, we heard your son on the drums again last night. He's getting good: great rhythm. Is it a passion of his?

Them: Yeah – I don't know how serious he is but he's certainly hoping to get into a full-time band.

You: Well, good luck to him. It's tough to make it to the top.

Them: Don't I know it, but it's important to encourage them at this age.

You: Yeah, sure – that's great parenting. On that issue, actually, I was going to ask a favour...

That's more like it!

Q **So what do you suggest for people like me who've got the grumpiest old man on the planet living next door?**

How did it go?

A *Well, there are neighbours from hell, of course, but with most people if you give them a bit of time, reach out to them a bit, you can get something of a decent relationship going. Go on, try it – surprise yourself.*

Q **No, honestly, it's *so* bad that it's getting the whole family down. Do you think we should just move?**

A *If you truly feel there is no way through, then fair enough. However, make sure you check out your new neighbours before you sign anything!*

29
When you need to influence a group

Can you really influence a group of people? In short, yes you can. And you'll often need to do it: at work, on holiday, at the kids' school.

Influencing groups is quite a different skill to one-on-one influencing. Often what we think we should do is the worst thing to do. However, it's not hard so you'll soon get the hang of it.

The local reading group has asked you to talk to a group of the members who are not using the group for reading discussions, just for gossip. Somebody needs to remind them of the purpose of the group. You've been chosen, but how on earth do you influence a group? A little differently, of course. But you can still do it.

Here's an idea for you... **Remember that, funnily enough, although it seems harder to sway a group, if you harness the group dynamics, it can be easier. If you've never seen the famous film *Twelve Angry Men*, go to the video store and rent it. It's about a murder trial where the jurors must reach a unanimous guilty or not guilty verdict. One of them isn't convinced. Watch it and you'll learn a lot about how to influence groups.**

This type of influencing challenge occurs frequently:

- The committee for Town Against The Superstore (TATS) has drifted into crazy anarchistic ideas, again. Time to bring them back to things objective.

- As head of the sixth form careers office, it's your responsibility to influence this group of young adults to invest more time and care in their university applications. And also, interestingly, influence one or two of them that university is not necessarily the way forward.

We need to influence groups more often than we think. So, what do we do? Clearly, we can't talk to everyone individually – that would take too long. If we open a discussion with the group as a whole there is a real danger we will lose control as we try and keep everybody happy. So: we choose a couple of main influencers. We build ideas using *and*. We flatter. We avoid the need for public put-downs. We appeal to the higher goal in us all. We help the group stay on track. And we stay positive. Let's take a look at each of those ideas.

Tip 1: Choose a couple of main influencers. Who are the main players in the audience? There are always one or two. Linda Smith of the reading group has the respect of the other ladies; win her over and the task will be easy. She likes you well enough, so what about a quiet cup of coffee with her a couple of days before the meeting? And what you do is be honest: ask for her support and help.

Tip 2: Use AND. When talking to the group, give the impression that you are building ideas by using 'and' rather than attacking ideas using 'but'. Thus: '... *and* one way I guess we could get the developers to think again is by not using a demo but simply shopping elsewhere.'

Tip 3: Flatter. Be positive about all ideas, as in '... that's certainly an option and I'm sure we might use it in the future – however, for now ...'

Tip 4: Appeal to the higher goal. And so '... could I perhaps just ask us to pause and remember that the essential idea here is what are you going to do beyond school and for your career. The answer is not automatically university.'

Tip 5: Help the group stay on track. With a lot of people talking at various times, it can be difficult to know what has been agreed and what has not. Ensure only one person talks at a time and try to get a flip-chart or white-board on which to summarise progress that everyone can see. If that's not possible, and you can only use your own pad, then stop and summarise every so often.

Tip 6: Stay positive. They will frustrate you, but you can get there if you keep your goal in mind. Be polite. Be persistent.

> **'Fewer things are harder to put up with than a good example.'**
> MARK TWAIN

Defining idea...

Q **I love these influencing ideas but I've got a problem – I get really nervous when I have to talk to groups and I'm sure I'd blow it. Is there anything I can do?**

A There are lots of techniques for the nervous. Here are some good basics. Be first in the room so you can greet everybody as they come in (then you will be talking to a roomful of friends). Rehearse by saying aloud in private the opening statements and key phrases you will need. Get a friend to be devil's advocate – worst questions possible – and make sure you can handle them. Stay on your feet and keep on the move: it helps with nervous energy. Wear 'easy' clothes (not brand new, uncomfortable shoes, for example). Have a flip-chart in the room to act as your sidekick and help you to 'keep track' of what's been said and agreed. Then you can 'relax' and manage the group.

Q **How will I know if I'm making progress or not?**

A Of course, it can be more difficult to know if you're getting through to a group rather than a single person. In a one-to-one conversation, you will be getting immediate feedback. Clues to look for with a group are: attentive body language (people leaning forward), nods of agreement, questions looking for clarification, good eye contact and some smiles from some of the audience at appropriate times. Positive Q&A sessions are also a sign that you've made an impact. You can intensify these by asking your own questions that look for positive answers.

30
Put it in writing

You don't know who you should meet. The person you need to talk to has been ducking your calls. Enough is enough. This needs to go into writing.

The building society statements simply do not make sense. Ruth's maths teacher is ignoring your calls. You are livid. Some serious 'in writing' influencing needs to be done.

If we can influence 'face to face', it's probably the best way to do it. It's 'live' and we can respond and get responses immediately. We can see the person and gauge their mood. We can get agreement. Overall, it's the best option.

However, there are times when we don't have that option or it isn't appropriate. That's when we need to use a letter or an e-mail – when it's formal (arguing the case that our son should be able to start his Easter holiday one week early because of his dad's shift work) or when it's complicated and we want to lay out all the points (why we want the shop to take away this washing machine and give us a brand new one and stop repeatedly trying to fix the 'old one') or when we need a 'paper trail' (and by that we mean when there may be questions and 'comeback'

Here's an idea for you...

When you write, before you put pen to paper or fingers to keyboard, use the classic 'W' questions: who (is it best to write to?); why (am I writing?); what (am I writing about and what do I want?); when (am I expecting a result?); where (will I get help with ensuring it is the best letter I can do?). If you answer all of those you should have a great letter.

concerning the nature of what you said/they said etc.). So there are circumstances when a paper or electronic record is invaluable.

What's the best way to write this letter? The first suggestion is that you don't wait until you are 'in the mood'. One thing all professional writers learn early in their career is that if you wait 'until you are in the mood', not much gets written! Did you know that author Stephen King writes a novel in three months? He does that by writing 2000 words a day for 90 days, no break. Hey presto, 180,000 words.

So, let's pinch that idea and not mess about. Just write. And the faster you can get it written down the better. Get all your feelings down, get all the facts down, get all the failings down, and get it all down quickly. Don't worry: you can tidy up later. For now, we just want to capture everything.

Then we edit. This is when we get a flow so that we make the maximum impact. It goes without saying this is best done on a PC. We also need to take on board what makes a good letter.

It certainly has a *structure*. Make sure your letter has got a beginning, a middle and an end. The beginning is why you are writing (I am writing because I am very unhappy about the way my son was treated on the recent school trip). The middle is the facts

(He did in fact have a packed lunch but had chosen to eat it earlier; Mr Smith said …). The end is what you want (I would like an apology from Mr Smith to my son).

It has *flow*. Write naturally and don't be too formal (Re the apology which I am seeking in the first instance …), which simply creates unnecessary distance between you and the person you are trying to influence. Use your own 'voice'.

It has *balance*. You are much more likely to get them to listen if you represent both sides fairly (Of course, I know that my son is certainly no angel …).

Insist on *definite actions/requests and timescales*: I would like a response before the end of term …

Get another person to scan the document, just to make sure you haven't made some fundamental error. And ensure it has been grammar and spell checked (it's all available on the PC when you find the right pull-down menu). If it was a one-off hand-written letter, make sure you have a copy of it! Use appropriate paper and envelope because most people do open their own mail and first impressions do count.

Here's an important point if you're communicating by e-mail. If you send an e-mail, you may well need to confirm receipt. Call to check it has been received because spam filters may have blocked your message. It helps tremendously to choose your subject line carefully so it can be easily spotted (e.g. not 'REPLY needed' but 'GREEN SCHOOL: British Museum Trip June 2008').

'What a lot we lost when we stopped writing letters. You can't re-read a phone-call.'
SOMERSET MAUGHAM

Defining idea…

How did it go?

Q **I've never been able to write so how will I go about influencing by letter or e-mail?**

A   Start by challenging the belief that you can't write. Where did it come from? Some unhelpful teacher at school? Probably. You can write. It's just that you can't write like Hemingway or Dickens. But you can write. It's just you probably haven't practised for a while. To write you need to (1) believe you can write – and you can – and (2) write. So (1) is sorted, move on to (2) and start writing.

Q **I personally like hand-written letters. Is it okay if I write instead of type or will other people expect a printout of some kind?**

A   We don't see enough handwriting now and a hand-written letter can be very powerful. Let's summarise. Good points: impact, personal, shows you have made an 'effort'. And it's still the only way in very 'personal' situations such as love and romance or ill-health. Not so good: you'll probably need to draft the letter on a PC then copy it out, it can look 'weak' or 'outdated' (especially if you're writing to a corporate entity), you'll need to make a photocopy, and, finally, you can't re-send so easily if your letter is lost as you can with an e-mail. Overall, though, hand-written letters can be powerful in the right circumstances.

31

Be honest

It's sometimes tempting to stretch the truth to increase our influencing power – just like politicians do. However, don't: it will only come back to bite you.

When you're wondering how to increase your influencing power without cheating, you can actually use your 'squeaky-clean' honesty as a major asset.

Think back to a younger you, a much younger you. At junior school. The you who said 'she pulled my hair!'; who said 'he kicked the ball through the window!'. Only she/he didn't – you lied! Why did we do that? We wanted the situation to be resolved quickly, we wanted to influence at speed. We wanted *maximum* impact. The only trouble is of course we were lying. Sally had not pulled our hair. And Vipul was nowhere near the ball when it went through the window.

Back then, we were too young to know better – and, to a certain extent, children have to lie to get a better understanding of what is 'right'. Also back then, we didn't have the brilliant ideas we're collecting now for proper influencing.

Here's an idea for you... **Imagine you are wearing the world's best lie detector. Run through the points that you are going to make and imagine your lie detector assessing what you're saying: red equals clear and blatant lie; amber, a bit 'dodgy'; green, plain truth. As you rehearse your argumentation in your head, you really need that indicator to stay green.**

In any influencing situation we can get rapidly to a resolution if the weight of evidence is overwhelming and/or we are skilful. As a child we don't have the skills so we go the evidence route. And if we don't have the evidence, we make it up. And, as you are only too aware, politicians are amongst the many who also often use this approach. And you know what *always* happens to them.

So, what should our strategy be? It should always be to stick to the truth when influencing and be incredibly skilful with what we have. And just to be clear why we should:

- We will be found out, and that doesn't just spoil the current discussion, it tends to tarnish all discussions.
- It's hard to be skilful with lies because we begin to forget what we've said.
- Our personal reputation is damaged.

And to be doubly clear what we mean by a lie in influencing situations:

- Don't say 'I've never had a personal quarterly review' when actually it was only the last one that was cancelled.
- Don't say 'you've never looked at me like that' when actually what is annoying you is the wandering eye in the restaurant.
- Don't say 'you're the one who wastes our money' when you know you're just as bad.

So, a lie is not just a basic untruth ('I didn't "pad" my expenses'), it's also an exaggeration or generalisation that is clearly misleading ('I effectively did an MBA; it's just that personal circumstances meant I couldn't complete the final assessment').

Being scrupulously honest is, of course, very hard: deliberate vagueness, untruths and exaggeration all seem to be on the increase particularly in many business situations. Heard any of these? 'No – I didn't get your e-mail ...', 'That's odd, it went in the post straight away ...', 'She's not available this week ...', 'Didn't you see the internal advertisement for that role?', 'I had a bit of a personal crisis', 'The train was delayed', 'We were not aware of those market conditions ...'. Any of these could be true ... but.

If you show integrity wherever you can, you will be seen as a remarkably powerful influencer whether it is in a personal or business situation.

- Don't think a lie will help your influencing. At best it just puts off the point of judgement.
- Being truthful is highly effective in disarming the person you want to influence.
- Rationalising with 'white lie' argumentation will make others mistrust you.

'In a time of universal deceit, telling the truth is a revolutionary act.'
GEORGE ORWELL

Defining idea...

129

Q   **Most people agree that 'white lies' can be very helpful. Are you saying that's not the case?**

A   *Not necessarily. Most of us would perhaps refer to this as appropriate sensitivity. For instance, think of your friend who is going for an exam. You've tried to influence them to revise more but they haven't. They now anxiously ask you on the morning of the exam if you think they've prepared enough. The only answer from anybody with any humanity is 'yes: I'm sure it'll go well'. But, when the poor exam results come through and they again ask if you think they did enough revision, the answer is actually 'No'. It's a matter of timing. You wouldn't want them to be even more nervous before the exam but you must lead them to the truth after the fact.*

Q   **What about in a personal relationship? I'm sure my boyfriend keeps stuff from me. I'm not sure he would call it lying, but when we work on our finances, he always hesitates a bit.**

A   *Even in the most intimate and long-term relationship, we probably all have a right to – and need – our own space, our own bit of the world. In a loving relationship, a partner understands that. But in your situation here, then you do need to influence him – through your own absolute honesty – that such deceit is possibly detrimental to your long-term living and loving together, not to mention your financial security. For example, 'Look, I'm not sure what's going on here, but we agreed we would jointly save for a flat and we are both trying to put in as much money as we can. I just get a feeling that there's more money you have available. Now what's in your private account is your business, but could you at least tell me how committed you are to this?'*

32

Convince them to like you

It's so much easier to influence someone if they like you, of course, but what if it's a stranger you're dealing with? You'll need to make them like you quickly.

It is possible to create 'rapport' very quickly with anyone you meet. This is especially useful when you wish to influence somebody you've only just met.

Take 1: You're in the supermarket car park; you reverse; and you hit a car. Oh no! You step out of the car and find it's a friend's car you've hit. The conversation is not ideal – you are obviously uncomfortable about what you have done – but it is a civilised conversation because you know this person, she likes you and she knows this accident is not typical of you – it was just one of those things. She's more than willing to work with you to sort it out.

Take 2: You're in the supermarket car park; you reverse; and you hit a car. Oh no! You step out of the car and it turns out the car you've hit belongs to a big bloke with an angry stare. You are just about to apologise when he starts yelling at you. It's downhill from there. It ruins your day and it takes weeks to sort out because he is deliberately difficult and malicious at every turn of the paperwork.

In any influencing situation where the person doesn't seem to like you, make that the first challenge. Say to yourself I'm going to win this person over. When you make that decision, you'll find that you do win them over.

Of course, this is heavily stereotyped, but you get the point. It's generally easier to influence when we know somebody, and particularly when they like you. So, how do we speed up the influencing process with strangers we're meeting for the first time?

Here it is in a nutshell: be polite and be persistent. Follow these two guidelines and you will be there – quickly and easily. By 'be polite' we mean work with the person, don't rush to judge and ensure you don't alienate them. By 'be persistent' we mean keep going for what you want; don't be worn down.

Going back to the incident in the car park, here's an example of politeness and persistence in action:

Him: What the f**k have you done to my car? Weren't you looking where you were bloody well going?

You: I'm really sorry about that. What's the best way to sort this out? (Ignore the rudeness. With luck, you will never see this person again. You can't change what has happened, so don't dwell on the past. Be focused on the future; it *can* be changed.)

Him: You should have been more bloody careful in the first place.

You: (Resist the temptation to say 'obviously' in a voice dripping with sarcasm: stay out of the emotional minefield.) Shall we swap insurance details? I've got a pen and paper.

Him: (Beginning to calm down because there is nothing to 'bite on'.) What a way to start the day: I just popped in for some beer for the barbecue later.

You: Well, let's get this sorted, then we can both carry on with our days. The good news is both cars are still driveable.

Notice the politeness and persistence all the way through. Here are some tips on how to be polite:

- Use their name: it personalises. ('So, Peter, I think the key point here is ...')
- Thank them: it makes them feel appreciated. ('Great point, Sarah; how about ...')
- Use please: it shows them respect. ('Please will you explain that for me again ...')
- Use 'and' rather than 'but': it builds. ('And another option would be ...')
- Use 'as you know': it's respectful. ('As you are aware, there is a pay freeze at the moment ...')
- Look them in the eye and smile.
- Work hard to understand what they are saying and respect their views (even if you don't agree. ('So, let me try to explain that back to you and see if I have got it right. Ah, I'd never thought about it from that perspective before.')
- Take time. ('Let's arrange another meeting: I want to do this properly so that whatever we agree sticks'.)

To be persistent:

'I get by with a little help from my friends.'
THE BEATLES

Defining idea...

- Return to the facts. (So, John, I think the key facts are as follows ...')
- Agree things precisely. (To agree, then: in return for you working a longer notice period ...')
- Say no. ('I will have to say no. It's simply not possible to give a further discount.')
- Be assertive. ('Actually, that's not acceptable: I do need 30 minutes of your time before Friday. How can we make that happen?)

Q   Aren't some people just really unpleasant?

A   *Yes! But actually those people are few and far between. Most people might come over as unpleasant but they are in truth: just stressed, having a bad day, feeling bad because they know their car insurance has run out, already late for their meeting, etc. So, stay polite, stay persistent, and you will win them over.*

Q   If you are too 'nice', won't people take advantage of you or even get angrier because they really want a bit of a fight?

A   *You're right, of course. Sadly, some people do see 'politeness' and/or reasonableness as a sign of weakness. Not you, though. You see it as a strength and will stick to it. The important point is that being polite doesn't mean you allow yourself to be bullied; you are as tough an influencer as ever. Your second point is also a good one – some people do just want a fight. To manage that, think about your energy level. Match their anger energy with your politeness energy. Don't be polite and meek; be polite and strong. Whatever happens, they will soon see that you are not to be messed with.*

33

What was she wearing? Did you see his tie?

It's not that 'power-dressing' will win you the discussion, but dreary dress-sense could damage your credibility. It's worth working on this.

It won't take big money, or mean changing who you fundamentally are. Just a few easy-to-implement ideas will make sure you look the part.

Of course you should be able to express your individuality and of course it shouldn't matter, but wouldn't you:

- Think again about offering a salary increase to a key 'customer-facing' employee who was wearing a badly stained tie?
- Be unnecessarily distracted by a particularly short skirt when having a discussion about marketing strategy?
- Wonder why he's wearing odd socks with his sharp business suit?
- Think the lashings of perfume and extravagant hair-do was more suitable for a day at the races than a serious discussion about her ability to act as an executive coach?
- Be surprised that a wannabe reporter didn't have a pen to hand?

Here's an idea for you... **Try this, and you might even get away with it as a discussion in the pub. If you wanted to influence certain people and the 'first pass' of influencing would be a photograph of you, what clothes should you be wearing? Start with well-knowns such as Bill Gates, Richard Branson. Add a few of your own. Notice what people argue about ('no – simply because he's Richard Branson, that doesn't mean you could wear jeans') and what they do agree about ('yeah, okay, we'll agree on that – smart suit but no tie for Branson'). It will open your eyes to the huge breadth of appearance issues people notice.**

Yes, thought so. We're not saying it's fair: we're suggesting you should be pragmatic.

It's all about balance. Of course the influencing process can be well supported by what you wear. A smart suit to your business start-up discussion with the bank manager sounds ideal. Dress-down V-neck jumper and chinos on the shop-floor to talk to the warehouse staff about their demands seems perfect. Slacks and loose linen shirt to Friday's brain-storming off-site: excellent, just the right tone. And so on.

But don't take it too far. The essential message is that your appearance should support and not distract from your overall message. Consider the following. None can be absolutes of course, but they are worth considering.

These can help (for a man) and are often given insufficient attention.

- Great hygiene, especially hair (even more especially if it's long).
- Think very carefully about designer stubble. If you're a well-established designer/rock-star/male model, great. Everybody else: get a close shave.
- Suit and tie. If you're not a natural with dress-sense, at least find out which is the best colour for your build: e.g. grey or navy blue. And make sure it's pressed. Then get an interesting tie, but nothing from the joke shop.
- Polished shoes. Shoe care is definitely a common oversight.
- If casual, clean chinos, polo shirt, V-neck jumper and/or blazer can work well.

These can hinder (for a man):

- T-shirts. Only in the right environments (young/technical/not customer-facing).
- Torn jeans. Never!
- Tired suits. Never!
- Oily ties. Never!

These can help (for a woman):

- Simple: clean lines and non-fussy.
- Zero or minimal jewellery. Ditto for perfume.
- Colours that flatter your hair, shape and complexion. If you don't know, get advice.

'Do not trouble yourself much to get new things, whether clothes or friends ... Sell your clothes and keep your thoughts.'
HENRY DAVID THOREAU

Defining idea...

These can hinder (for a woman):

■ Too short a skirt.
■ Too revealing a top.
■ Too tight an outfit.
■ Too low a trouser band.

Plus try and get some variation on the 'easy' black city suit worn almost everywhere every day in some environments.

Remember that your appearance is not just about your clothes. The following can also reveal a lot about you: your pen, your notebook, your briefcase/bag, your purse/wallet. We've sometimes had these things so long that we have forgotten they are looking a little tired. And the shabby wallet bulging with receipts probably doesn't reflect a mind dedicated to organisation.

Q **So what about flirting: I do it all the time!**

A *This has strayed a bit from the main point of appearance but they are linked. Flirting, like seduction, is of course a form of influencing and involves your look. However, much as flirting is enjoyable, it should be restricted to the right settings. It would be a shame if it were said of you by your co-workers that you only got that promotion because you were such a flirt. So, use your personality and use your interpersonal skills, but don't flirt in crucial influencing situations.*

Q **I hear a lot about how certain colours and styles go well with certain skin tones and body shapes, and I have noticed that some days my clothes seem to look a lot better than others, but I don't really have a clue how it all works. Any suggestions?**

A *There's a lot in this. Probably the simplest way to get up to speed is to spend some time in a few clothes shops on a quiet day until you come across an assistant who's good at it – i.e. this skill of matching colour and style to skin and shape. There are plenty of them out there. Get them to show how a change of shirt colour has a big impression or a longer line of jacket makes you look taller. It's worth the effort because you can spend a lot of money on a piece of clothing that'll look great on someone else but – even though it's a lovely material and colour – will not do anything for you.*

How did
it go?

139

34

Ask, don't tell

Asking questions puts you in control. It gets the other person thinking differently and gives you thinking time – just what you want when you're trying to influence them.

We can't influence people if they don't digest our ideas properly and therein lies a problem. That person will possibly be resistant to our ideas and also too busy to hear us.

... Possibly distracted, too. Possibly tired as well. And possibly they're not sure whether they like us, or even whether they can trust us. So, how on earth do we get them to give us time so they can absorb the wisdom we have to offer? Easy: more *asking* and less *telling*. It works every time.

Although it seems obvious to tell people stuff – '... so here are three reasons why you should buy from us ...'/'... so, as I was saying, the current leasing arrangements must change because ...'/'... when you start at university, you should ...' – they only really digest that information if they trust us and they have a bit of time to reflect. However, when we are trying to influence someone, we may not have developed trust and they may well be short of time.

Here's an idea for you... **Think of the 'tells' you want to get across. Before you deliver them, jot them down on the left-hand side of a sheet of paper: (1) You need to give me a refund! (2) You need to decide between her or me! (3) We must move house! On the right-hand side, turn them into 'asks': (1) What do you think would be an appropriate level of refund considering the problems you have caused me? (2) How do you think I feel, being unsure of where your affections lie? (3) What do you think we can do to get more space now the children need their own rooms? Deliver the 'asks' and you'll be one step ahead before you really get started.**

A simple and effective way to overcome this challenge is to ask questions. When we ask a question, it causes someone to pause; it causes them to reflect; and, importantly, the process of asking questions ensures someone feels more respected, which gives the natural opportunity to build trust. Compare these:

- A reasonable rent is 1500 (tell). Did you decide that 1500 is a reasonable rent? (ask).

- It's disgusting the way you leave the flat in such a mess (tell). How do you think I feel when I get no help with tidying? (ask).

- You must do more revision (tell). What do you think makes the difference between an A and an A*? (ask).

The former has lower impact. The latter has higher impact. The former simply reinforces the natural resistance to us being influenced. The latter gets us to 'wake up' and think about the issue in a different way. 'Ask' treats people in a more 'consultative' manner; treats them as adults; treats them with respect; and appears less dictatorial. It's not magic, of course, but it's a brilliant idea to add to your influencing portfolio; it's another approach that increases your chances of success in having it your way.

A further bit of fine-tuning you can do is to remind yourself of something you intuitively know, but you also know is often forgotten in the heat of a big influencing discussion. There are questions that are *open* and there are questions that are *closed*.

Open questions encourage conversation – 'So, how will you raise the deposit, do you think?' 'What are you really looking for in your next financial adviser?'

Closed questions angle for a simple 'yes' or 'no' answer or a one-word response – 'How much money do you have to spend on a new car?' 'Will you resign if you don't get your salary demand?'

Both types of question are powerful when you begin to use them deliberately rather than accidentally. They can get you to the decision you want more quickly.

'A definition is the start of an argument, not the end of one.'
NEIL POSTMAN, US media critic

Defining idea...

Q How do I run the conversation now that it's a series of questions rather than just me telling them what I need? It seems to me that it'll be a lot harder to manage the direction of the interaction.

A *The nice thing is that it should feel more like a normal conversation and if you relax into that and stay attentive it'll be fine. Clearly you cannot know how somebody will reply to your questions, but at least you know that they are engaged with the discussion, which of course is much of the battle. With a 'tell', you don't have that reassurance because you are not getting regular feedback. Every response to one of your questions is feedback that lets you know if you're making progress or not. Also, remember that because you are not telling, you have more of an opportunity to listen and think, and hence decide the best direction to take next. You'll soon get used to it and never want to go back to your old ways.*

Q Isn't there a danger of giving them too much say – getting them to feel they do have a view, and not the view you're trying to steer them towards?

A *There is always a danger of doing things badly, but you won't do that if you're careful and focused on what you want. Your boyfriend does have a say in the ongoing flat tidiness issue. As far as you're concerned he's a 'slob'; as far as he's concerned you are a control freak. These are two valid views on Mars and Venus. Influencing will only happen if you talk it through properly; and that is best done with lots of asking and listening rather than telling and yelling. Ask him how long he thinks the DVD drive will last if it's trying to play disks covered with grime.*

35

Slow down: achieve more

It's very difficult to influence in a hurry. In fact, almost by definition, 'hurry-up influencing' fails. Slow things down and you'll achieve a whole lot more.

Have you ever tried to 'sort someone out' really quickly — like a ten-minute talk on binge drinking with your teenage daughter at breakfast? You'll have noticed that it tends not to go that well.

If you catch your boss in the corridor and try to influence him on a major new product issue, what are your chances of succeeding? Close to none. You see, you simply can't be 'efficient' with people: you can't say 'right, let's get this customer complaint sorted in the next 10 minutes'. It may be theoretically possible but, human nature being what it is, it will probably require more time – certainly if the resolution is going to 'stick'. And to 'force the answer' will probably cause it to 'bounce back at some later stage'.

Here's an idea for you...

Start choosing rather than reacting. If someone is irritating, do you have to be irritated? No. If you're under pressure and a decision is needed by the end of the day, does it help to shout at your assistant? No. It's not always straightforward to make more helpful responses rather than just reacting negatively but it is something you can practise. As you get better at it, you'll see that it's worth the effort because you will find it easier to influence in the trickier situations.

Here are some useful tips from people who are good at influencing:

■ *Take it slow.* Talk at a normal pace. Write notes. Listen to every point. Be in the moment. The more you get clarified and corrected now, the easier it will be in the long term.

■ *Be in there for the 'long haul'.* There is often a bigger issue lurking and it's best to find out what this is, so don't be too quick in deciding that you've reached the conclusion.

■ *Give them time.* It's unreasonable to expect an immediate response from someone, especially on a complex issue.

■ *Don't allow yourself to be rushed.* 'Yes, I agree we need a quick decision. But it won't really be quick if it's not the correct one, so let's take a bit more time to get it right.'

If you're rushing and you're anxious, it can severely reduce your influencing power. But how do we remain calm and focused? One effective answer is to learn how to meditate. Let's look at how to carry out a simple breathing meditation.

Aim at meditating for ten minutes each morning and each evening. The morning meditation complements your sleep and sets you up for the rest of the day. The evening meditation ensures you have a revitalised evening and that you sleep well. Try to meditate at least once every day. It's a proactive mechanism, a bit like brushing your teeth.

To actually meditate, sit quietly in a comfortable chair. Choose a location that will be quiet and undisturbed, but don't bother trying to find somewhere that's absolutely silent because you probably won't find it. Focus on your breathing and allow your mind to get a little quieter and your body to relax. Thoughts *will* come into your mind, but return your awareness to your breathing. Don't try not to have thoughts; simply maintain a focus on your breathing.

Some meditations will be very relaxing, some very turbulent. It is often the latter which are the most helpful. Try not to judge the experiences you have during meditation; just accept that they are what your mind and body need at that moment.

Above all, as one of the great meditation teachers said: don't worry about what happens in your meditation – it's what happens outside your meditation that is most important. And as you regularly meditate, you will notice significant change.

Once you can, extend your meditation time from ten to fifteen to twenty minutes per session.

Let's not be cynical on this. Apply an open mind and genuinely try it out. You'll be amazed at how calm and focused your influencing becomes.

'Do less, achieve more.'
From the mantra of the business gurus

Defining idea...

147

Q **But sometimes you have just got to get stuff done, especially in the world of business. Why should I slow down?**

A *So true. But, as you know, it's surprising how much of the stuff we 'just get done' comes back to bite us when it later unravels. For a piece of influencing to be successful, we must get two kinds of agreements. First is the physical agreement – that's the signature on the contract or the verbal 'will do' from the horse's mouth. But then we must also get the emotional okay: the signal that they are really committed; that they understand what they are letting themselves in for. And that latter takes time. People need time to absorb an idea, feel fairly treated, get their head around the implications. Once again: there is no such thing as 'hurry-up' influencing. Accept that the best agreements need time, but that time invested will be recouped many times later on if you get an agreement that sticks. The garage never messes you about again. Your mum stops making such comments in front of your children. And the building society manager sends you a personal card every Christmas.*

Q **But don't you agree that some people are procrastinators?**

A *Okay, yes. So we need to balance the time for reflection that we've been discussing with the necessity for action. Whenever we close a stage of a process of influencing, always close on an action – 'Brilliant, I think we have made really good progress on the plans for the new house extension. I'm glad we have begun to convince you that we would like a more ecological approach but we do not see why that should be so expensive. Shall we agree that you will get back to us in five days with an initial new quote?'*

36

Give and take

It'll help you a lot in getting what you want if you are willing to give a little. Be flexible and reasonable and you'll discover it works wonders.

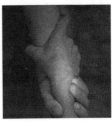

From the beginning of time, people have traded to get to a beneficial outcome for both parties. That's actually what we're doing with great influencing

Generally, when we're influencing we are taking something from someone: we influence them to be more tidy; they feel that takes away their freedom to be messy. We influence someone to give up smoking; they feel we have taken away one of their last simple pleasures. We influence the school to allow our daughter to not attend speech day because of a family commitment; they feel we have taken away their authority with the children.

When we take something away from someone – however reasonable it might be to do so – they can easily feel resentful. Consequently, a good approach when influencing is if we take something from someone – be it their aversion to tidying, their smoking or their authority – we also give something back in return.

Here's an idea for you...

Take a small pack of those yellow stickies. Quickly write down what you want. Put each want on a separate yellow sticky and then put them up one part of the wall. Now do the same with all the possible gives you can identify. Stick those on another part of the wall. Now line them up, where you think there are equivalences. For example, with the architect, every 1% discount gets an hour of your coaching time. When you're done, transfer all the stickies to your notebook. You're now ready for a great give-and-take influencing discussion.

So that's the brilliant idea: when you take something away, work hard to give something back in return. Thus, although we ask them (and they agree) to be more tidy generally, we agree we will no longer be concerned about the state of their study. We ask them to give up smoking; in return we agree to help them with their writing, as one of the reasons they smoke is to help them stay at their desk and write. We ask the school to be flexible, we agree we'll man a stand at the next fund-raising day, showing that we are very much loyal parents.

It's not difficult and it can even be fun to develop your give-and-take approach. Here are some tips to get you going in the right direction.

Firstly, before any influencing even starts, you think about what you *might* be able to give. For example:

- You *want* tidiness from your girlfriend; you could *give* by doing more cooking (of which you do hardly any at the moment).
- You *want* more discount from the architect; you could *give* him an introduction to a couple of friends who are looking for a good architect.
- You *want* a book deal; you will *give* a guarantee of so many books sold.

Then, when the influencing starts, be alert to give-and-take opportunities. For instance, imagine that you start talking about your 'want' of tidiness, but then you realise the real issue is about your lack of interest in the theatre, one of her passions. So you 'give' a commitment to go once a month and begin to learn a lot more about her kind of theatre.

When you start talking to the architect about your 'want' of a discount, you realise the last thing he wants is more customers because he's simply too busy. Instead, though, you can coach him on his presentation skills because he is very nervous of doing large presentations but, as a sales director, you have become very skilled at them.

If the influencing is particularly serious (say as in business or with the builders), once you have identified your gives and takes, decide their relative worth. Thus, a day of your time may be worth two days of their time. It may take two hours per week to tidy the flat but at least one hour per day to do the cooking and shopping.

Before starting your influencing try to have as long a list of gives and takes as possible. Otherwise you might find that the whole process grinds to a halt too early.

'The most important thing in any relationship is not what you get but what you give.'
ELEANOR ROOSEVELT

Defining
idea...

How did
it go?

Q But they are plain wrong. Why should I give them anything?

A *Sure. They cancelled the flight and you wasted the first day of your holiday. They are in the wrong. So give them your politeness (by the way, that doesn't mean you are weak or soft; just polite). Most people in that situation will be rude and aggressive. However, when you treat the airline staff as human beings your demands are much more likely to be met. See, there is always something you can give.*

Q In my situation, I don't have much to give. Are there any tips on making what I do have seem more valuable, so that when I do give it, it's appreciated more?

A *Good question. In general, simply because you are willing to give something, don't diminish its value by giving it away too easily (e.g. by saying 'oh, it's nothing; you can have that'). That'll worry the other person into thinking they should have got more out of you. So, follow these guidelines. Only give something if you get in return ('Okay, I'll do the 2 a.m. radio show but I want it guaranteed in writing that I get first option on the 5 p.m. drive-time show when it next comes up'). Give small (you could offer to cover all the shifts: start with one, though). Give slowly (don't say straight away you don't need the free car-parking slot because you don't drive). Build value (you don't just know how to do presentations: you are rated number one presenter in your company).*

152

37

What are your priorities?

What do you want to start with? What can be left until another day? What's *really* important here? Then that's where your effort should be focused.

Also ask if there's any underlying principle that needs to be established. What might not really matter as long as this one thing has been seen to?

Here's a story to get you thinking. For many months, a group of managers had been travelling through a dense jungle. A routine had been established: get up early, spend the day hacking through the jungle, set up camp, cook the evening meal, sleep, get up and do it again. And again. To break the monotony, there were occasional training courses on how to sharpen the machetes. But basically things were much the same. In fact, most of the managers no longer knew where they were and what they were trying to do. They just seemed to have one mission in life: keep hacking.

Of course, some of the managers occasionally asked questions, sometimes while hacking along, but especially after supper around the campfire when their faces were a little hidden in the shadow. But in the end, it would always come back to the

Here's an idea for you... **When you face the task of getting your way with several parties who are interconnected in some way, think of the priority that could amplify your influencing. That's the one to focus on. For instance, imagine you're having an extension done but you can't seem to get your tradesmen to get the finishing touches done. The plumber has disappeared without moving the last of the pipework into the runs where they should be and despite your nagging, the electrician hasn't returned to add the final sockets. Plus you need to book the plasterers. Make it a priority to get a date for the plastering. They can't do their stuff if the others haven't finished so they will join you hassling the plumber and electrician. Sorted!**

announcement: we're making progress, gentlemen. And then the official number of kilometres covered would be read out. And it was impressive.

One morning, one young manager decided he had had enough of the seemingly aimless hacking. He decided to climb as high as he could. He chose the tree carefully and he exchanged his boots for trainers. He left his pack on the ground and just strapped a bottle of water to his belt. It was tough: the canopy was dense and at every level there were different insects, birds and monkeys that startled him. But, as he climbed, the air was definitely getting cleaner, the light was looking brighter and then, suddenly, the most glorious experience: he broke through the tree canopy. It was as if his head had broken through the surface of the ocean from below. A glorious rising sun greeted him. But he was also shocked to the core. He shouted to his colleagues who were starting to set off. At first they couldn't hear him, but then the words came through loud and clear: *wrong jungle!*

You get the point, of course: they had lost the plot. And sometimes we need to remind ourselves what the plot is. Is it really about you being late to the meeting or is this discussion really about the way your boss talks to you? Is this really about the cost of wine or that too much alcohol is being consumed? Is this discussion really about her homework or whether the school is even the right one for her?

To keep a firm grasp of that plot it's essential that everybody understands what the priority is. All concerned should know what is and what isn't really important.

To put it another way: you can only really have it your way if you really, really know what is having it your way.

So, where do you start your influencing when the job just isn't as promised at the interview? You don't have a dedicated assistant as was promised, you are not really responsible for EMEA, etc. ... You go back to the person who offered you the job and discussed the contract and job specification with you. Get that sorted and all else will follow ...

And then you want your husband to take up a healthier lifestyle. After all there is so much he could do .... You start with something really easy, such as a daily fifteen-minute brisk walk. He'll then start feeling better and be willing to work on his diet, cut down on alcohol ...

In general when looking for what is really important, look for what will help you have it your way: make it general rather than specific, long term rather than short term, easy rather than complicated.

'**Often we are so busy with sawing that we forget to sharpen the saw.**'
STEPHEN COVEY, business author

Defining idea...

155

How did it go?

Q But I want it all! Why shouldn't I aim for that?

A *You can have it all but you still need a starting point. What you've got to discover is what the priority is; what is the big thing that will also allow the rest to be solved? Then you will get it all your own way. With the landlord who's constantly letting you down, focus all your initial energies on the tenancy contract. Get him to give you a guarantee that he will live up to his end of the agreement. Then you can address the idea of replacing the fridge. Then the rubbish shower. And so on.*

Q But isn't it better to 'work up' to the big picture; get the landlord to do each little job in turn?

A *It's a possibility. But then you will simply have to continue the process: endless, little frustrating influencing jobs. What we want to do is one big influencing job: get it sorted out once and for all. So, although you might be worried about your chances of success, it's probably a better process overall.*

38

The facts, just the facts

If in doubt, get the facts. If doubt creeps in again, return to the facts. Then you'll succeed. You need to learn what the relevant facts are and how to get them.

Influencing has two ingredients: facts and emotion. Both play a big part in helping you get what you want. Let's get good at the facts part.

What are facts: facts are your evidence. The bigger, better and stronger they are, the more likely you are to have it your way. If you then overlay a good emotional story, too, you are on to a winner.

■ If you want a 4% pay increase and you can show that other people in a similar position have received such an increase … well … your influencing will be easier.

■ If you want to influence your partner, who has recently had a heart attack, to reduce fat in their diet and you are able to produce four recent, well-documented studies that show categorically how fat reduction in the diet is essential … well … your influencing will be easier.

Here's an idea for you...

When presenting facts as part of your influencing, ensure that your language and tone reinforce the fact that it *is* a fact you are presenting. Quoting a supporting reference can be effective here. You could say, 'We should be reading to the children every night if we want to help them in the long term, rather than letting them watch the TV until it's time for bed.' But you'll add impact if you can add validation: 'It says in *New Scientist* that children's linguistic skills are improved by reading bedtime stories with them. Don't you think we should do that more with our kids and turn the TV off earlier?'

■ If you want to influence your business partner on the sales and marketing benefits of starting a blog, you need data, hard facts.

You get the point. But where do you get the facts from? The good news is that now, with the internet, it's really easy. But that's not even the full story. Here are some great sources for facts.

The internet. Search engines such as Google and MSN Search will rapidly bring up pages and pages of information – sometimes way too much. Try using 'advanced search' facilities to reduce the amount of information produced. Online reference sources are available from specialised sources for your own field/s, as well as general encyclopaedias such as Encyclopaedia Britannica and Wikipedia. Much comment has been made about how a lot of info that's available on the internet is not fully validated, nor assembled by people with proper research backgrounds. That's probably very true. However, the internet does allow rapid cross-referencing so that concern can probably be ignored.

Other people. Whatever the subject on which you need data, there will be other people you know who know what you need. And you can ask them questions: How do you defend your price? What does your landlord charge you? How on earth did you convince your boyfriend to reduce booze expenditure? What made your company start recycling seriously? The key thing here is that during any later influencing process you need to be able to avoid the explicit or implicit accusation that, 'of course the facts would say that – you obtained them'. So, choose a large, random sample of people and keep all of the records.

Formal data gathering. Of course, there are occasions where the data you need – e.g. the specific benefits of recycling for your organisation or the impact of product withdrawal for your company – are not available in the public domain and so commissioning a research company might be a good solution. In this case, the important thing is to 'reverse engineer' what you are looking for. For instance, 'We need data to convince the board of directors that environmentally beneficial packaging materials are now essential. They will be concerned about the cost increase, which for the first year is significant. So we need data that show the increased cost will be compensated for by (1) specific extra sales, (2) a better public image within the first twelve months and (3) a gain of market share in the long term. So, what questions do we need to ask?'

'All we want are the facts, ma'am.'
Dragnet

Defining
idea...

159

How did it go?

Q **I want to convince my husband that the children should not be watching so much TV and playing video games for so long at such an early age. I can find plenty of comment and opinion to back me up, but where do I get some hard facts?**

A *You are right: it's important to distinguish between comment and facts. There will be plenty of scientific data for you to access if you refine your search. Try adding the word 'facts' or 'data' to every online search or experiment with the advanced search facility in your search engine. Or you could switch to a different search engine for variety.*

Q **I presented comparative salary data to my boss and she said 'no' to the raise I wanted: 'Well, we can't afford that and anyway working in a market town like this is much more pleasant than commuting to the city every day.' What do I do now if the facts haven't worked?**

A *There are two points here. You aren't comparing like-for-like: the pay in the city is higher to compensate for extra travel and housing costs. And your employer is making a valid point: what value do you put on quality of life? Only you can say. Facts do not always guarantee success, but they are a brilliant tool to make being a successful influencer more likely.*

39

Thank

A really genuine 'thank you' costs you nothing and makes the other person feel good even though you might have wrung a tough concession out of them.

And even if you don't get what you want, thank them for listening to you and giving their time. It could make it much easier when you get a second chance.

Saying 'thank you' is seriously important because all influencing is an emotional experience as well as an exchange of data and information: if we treat someone well, they cannot help but be more likely to be swayed by our thoughts. This idea is sometimes known as 'managing the emotional bank account'. Like with our financial bank accounts, it helps if we make regular deposits and keep withdrawals down to the bare essentials.

Deposits into the emotional bank account are: politeness ('thank you'), courtesy ('just to let you know, I'll be 10 minutes late'), engagement (know the other person's name, switch off your mobile phone), following up (sending a summary e-mail after the meeting), good time-keeping (be there when you said you would), and connecting (shaking hands, making eye contact, open body language, a smile).

Here's an idea for you...

Have a 'thank you' day. Whatever happens, try very hard to thank people. Look for something you can thank them for and look them in the eyes as you do it. At the garage, as you retrieve your credit card, look them in the eyes and thank them. With your boss, after all the negative feedback he's given you, look him in the eyes and say 'thank you, that was helpful'. You'll be rewarded with a look that tells you you've done something special.

As well as 'none of the above', withdrawals from the emotional bank account are not being loyal (going behind people's backs) and lying ('I was promised this would happen' … when you weren't!).

So 'thank you' is wider than the words. It's respecting someone's time and their thoughts. It's listening carefully to someone. It's being loyal. A 'thank you' approach helps that other person feel good, and if they feel good they are more likely to want to work with you and be receptive to your influencing.

Make a deliberate effort to connect with people you wish to influence. 'Old-school' recommendations are often about staying 'detached' and 'cold' when trying to influence. That's a very old-fashioned and confrontational style, especially in business today. Connect! This connection in business can be formalised into your influencing network.

This influencing network contains not only people you sometimes need to influence, but also people who will help you influence. Imagine how great it would be to have the ability to say, 'I'd like you to speak to Sally; she's someone I've known and worked with for several years; she knows a lot about this sector of the market and I think she will reassure you that we would make an excellent partner for you.'

And as your influencing network grows, this builds your 'brand': who you are and what you stand for. Just as a commercial brand will influence you or not, your personal brand will support your influencing or not. Imagine how pleasant it would be if you got this phone message: 'You don't know me, but I'm heading a new division of the business and before we start looking externally I wanted to talk to you. I have a head-count and I have a generous package and I am looking for the absolute best people. Your name keeps coming up. I wondered if you would like an off-the-record conversation later. Or we could meet any time tomorrow if that's convenient.'

Remarkable as it may seem, the building of your brand starts with simple 'thank yous'! If you want a reminder of the impact of thanking, learn 'thank you' in other languages for when you are travelling. They may be the only words you know, but you'll feel the benefit of being able to say *muchas gracias* – or whatever – in the taxi, at the hotel and after the meeting. That's all it takes to show you are trying and that will win people over quicker.

'The grateful mind is constantly fixed upon the best. Therefore it tends to become the best. It takes the form or character of the best, and will receive the best.'
WALLACE D. WATTLES, motivational guru

Defining idea...

163

Q **Doesn't being gushingly friendly and grateful make you look weak and, worse, insincere?**

A *There is a difference between being passive – which is, of course, not respecting your own rights – and being friendly. If you are passive, you are being weak. If you are being friendly, you can be strong. Here's friendly:*
You: Morning, Tom. Good to see you again; how's things?
Tom: Good, good.
You: Excellent. So we need to pick up on our discussion about how we can get distribution costs down. I very much want to get this to work for both of us. Happy to continue?
Tom: Sure: why don't you kick off?

Here's passive (and the collision course to failure):
Tom: So, our agenda is to review costs again?
You: If that's okay by you.
Tom: Well, it's not what we want but I think if we don't you're threatening us with taking the business away.
You: It's not quite like that ...
Tom: Whatever, let's get on with it.

Q **What if they don't return my efforts and it's all 'withdrawals' from my emotional bank account?**

A *Say something about it! 'Look, I know neither of us is happy about the redundancy proposals, but it would make things a lot easier if, first, we were more civilised to each other in this room and, second, we didn't talk about what was happening outside this room until we have full agreement. Can I have that agreement?'*

40

Listen – really listen

Why isn't your influencing working? What are their objections? Listen carefully and you will understand. Then you'll get a better chance of having it your way.

What exactly is their point of view? Why are they so resistant? Why don't they seem to be able to 'get it'? If you hear what they're saying, you'll figure it out.

Have you ever become thoroughly fed-up with someone in a discussion, especially if it's getting really heated and turned into a full-blown argument? Did you say, 'You're not listening to me?' It's *so* frustrating, because we know that if only they'd listen properly, we would get that breakthrough essential to what we want to achieve.

But, of course, not only are they not listening to us, *we are not listening to them.* The more passionate we are about the subject we are discussing, the closer we are to the reasons for influence and the more the dangers of not listening.

The influencing process has to be a two-way thing: we tell, they listen; they tell, we listen. We comment on each other's views; we refine our views; we come to an agreement.

Here's an idea for you... **Enhance your listening skills whenever you can. If you're in a face-to-face situation, really observe the other person's face rather than taking loads of notes, or looking at PowerPoint slides or your laptop. On the phone, take key-point notes by making a point of asking for 'explain back' confirmation – 'have I got this right?'. Both of these techniques will make you a better listener.**

So, to be a good influencer, we have to be good listeners. How do we become better listeners?

■ Informally you can just try this: write LISTEN in block capitals at the top of every page in your influencing note pad. Acting as a constant reminder, it can work surprisingly well.

■ More formally, you can agree to take it in turns to explain your side of the story, with the proviso that neither of you interrupts until the other has finished speaking.

■ More formally still, the above process can be followed by the requirement that the listener 'explains back', to the speaker's satisfaction, what he/she has just said. This latter process, it has to be said, seems easy but it's actually very hard. However, it is an amazingly powerful technique. Much conflict resolution and excellent influencing can be carried out by 'listening to understand'.

■ Taking breaks is another important strategy. As we discuss, influence and argue, we get tired and, often, stressed. Both states make us poorer listeners.

■ Remove distractions such as incoming e-mail prompts, open-plan environments, other people talking at the same time, personal worries.

■ Prepare for the discussion so it does not take you long to 'acclimatise' to what is being said. Read any briefing notes carefully ahead of time and plan out your case.

Don't forget the personal preparation – take a breather beforehand to clear your head.

'Two ears and one mouth: that's the ratio in which they should be used.'
EPICTETUS, in essence

Defining idea...

How do you get them to become a better listener?

- By being a better listener yourself – your behaviour will influence them.

- By asking them to listen and 'explain back' at regular intervals.

Try this as a useful skill-development exercise with a friend to help him/her prepare for some important influencing they need to do – or, if you are in business, with a team in which you can get people to pair up.

Either way, choose a topic over which the sides differ (or if it is a team exercise you might give out differing business views: a classic one, of course, is company view versus customer view). In each pairing the speaker has a timed four minutes to explain their view. During that time, the listener cannot interrupt; he or she must just listen. At the end the listener needs to explain it back – to the speaker's satisfaction. Things to look for are:

- *Essential details:* did they mention in what way the product was broken, how long they had been waiting, whose birthday it was?
- *Any subtle points:* what was their real worry?
- *Timing of explanation compared with the original 4 minutes:* what ratio; did they just take two minutes, for example?

The exercise can be made more sophisticated with the use of a tape-recorder for 100% accuracy and/or a third person as an impartial observer. It's great fun and really helps develop everyone's listening skills immensely.

169

Q   **What do you do with the person who just will *not* listen?**

A   *Before we get into the answer, consider this. Sometimes people ask this question because they are not getting their way and they assume that the listener has not recognised the brilliance of what's been said. Actually the listener may fully understand what the speaker has said, but just not like the idea. It's worth bearing in mind. However, if you are convinced they are just an awful listener then use the 'explain back' approach – ask them to sum up what you've said. Point out that they are not listening by giving at least two examples of facts they clearly didn't hear. And finally, if you're still getting nowhere, find someone who will listen, such as their boss.*

Q   **I like the idea of 'playing-back' to show you understand, but what about when the meeting isn't very long and time is short? How can you deepen understanding rapidly?**

A   *Understanding is vital to good influencing, especially in business, and even more especially in complex deals. An easy thing to do that's often neglected is to send briefing notes before the meeting. These should be of 'executive summary' style – just the very essence of the subject, which allows someone to absorb the key points quickly. It should be made clear that it is mandatory that people read these before the meeting. One tip is to start the meeting by going round the table asking people for a thirty-second summary of the document. Not only does that get everyone's head into gear, it reveals those who haven't done their homework. They'll do it next time!*

41

Learn, learn, learn

You're going to be living with those teenagers for a long time yet. By learning what does and doesn't work when influencing them, you'll have an easier time of it.

You want to be happy; you want to be lucky in love; you want to be wealthy. It's all about influencing. Successful influencers can have it all.

Only problem about influencing is that they don't teach it at school, or college. The best you might get is one of those overblown 'negotiation skills' courses, which will teach you how to shave 37% off the cost of an oil-rig. So we must decide to learn the skills for ourselves.

You will want to be able to influence quicker and more easily, and with a group rather than just one person, and with people whose native tongue is not English, and with people who are cynical and people who have got a bus to catch. You can influence them all by first becoming brilliant at the basics and then continuing to learn.

Here's an idea for you...

Decide that you will learn how to influence someone you love, brilliantly with affection. You will learn to influence your boss, brilliantly with elegance. You will learn to influence your bank manager, brilliantly with skill. And decide you're going to learn all this within six calendar months of now. If you set yourself a specific challenge with a target completion date it will give you the discipline to make sure you succeed.

You probably won't be perfect at this stuff straight away, but you will be more than good enough to get started on the right path. And you can make it easier and easier by learning. Every time you go into an inflencing discussion with your teenage son, notice what works and notice what doesn't work. Then do more of the former and less of the latter.

Here are the sort of things you're looking for in the person:

- Timing: is it best discussed immediately or later?
- Tone: what sort of voice works – firm or more gentle?
- Is it best discussed on a walk, down the pub or formally?

And when are you at your best:

- When you have some notes?
- 'On the fly'?
- First thing in the day?

So, how do you become a learner and how do you become even better at influencing? For starters, review every important influencing session, whether at work or home. Analyse the interaction and identify where things worked well and what didn't get you anywhere.

Keep notes. In fact, start your own influencing book. Buy a nice notebook specifically for the purpose and jot down key tips that work for you.

A really brilliant idea is to spend time with people who are great at influencing. Notice how they talk to the sales assistant about returning the jumper; notice how they talk to the supplier about the quality issue. What makes them so good? What do they say and what do they do? A top tip is to actually observe them first hand rather than just asking them 'what do you do?' – they may not really know.

When you spend time with people who are good influencers, what you should especially look for is what they do that you don't do (but soon will). Keep a note of everything.

Compare these two:

Colleague: So how did your discussion about increasing the head-count go?

You: Rubbish! The guy's an idiot. Doesn't listen; I'm going to look for another job.

'*The most important thing any teacher has to learn, not to be learned in any school of education I ever heard of, can be expressed in seven words: learning is not the product of teaching. Learning is the product of the activity of learners.*'
JOHN HOLT, *Growing Without Schooling*

Defining idea...

175

Colleague:	Well, it's a great job you've got, you know. Good salary and car.
You:	Yeah, but the guy's holding me back. He's not an out-of-the-box thinker like me.
Colleague:	Well, I don't know … wouldn't it be worth another conversation with him?
You:	No – that would just be weak on my part.

Colleague:	So how did it go?
You:	Reasonable: I've got an agreement to a further discussion pending me finding more relevant data.
Colleague:	Oh – so at least he's listening, is he?
You:	Well, that's my job really. He's a busy guy. I want the head-count; hence I need to convince him!
Colleague:	Yeah, I guess that's true.
You:	Another hour's work and I think I'll have something he can't argue with. Great learning curve for me: I should have checked some data before I walked into his office today.
Colleague:	Well, you can't anticipate everything every time!
You:	Maybe not, but I can get better every time.

Whose career will go further? Who would you prefer as a colleague? Working for you? As your boss? Quite. Be a learner. Start now.

Q   How can I measure my success at influencing?

A   Clearly not by whether you 'win' every discussion. But when you walk away ask yourself a series of questions. Did you do everything you could do? Are you pleased with your performance? If there is one thing you would do differently what would it be? If an impartial external observer were commenting on your performance, what would he/she say? And if you are satisfied, or more than satisfied, with those responses, you count it as successful.

Q   What are the characteristics of the best influencers?

A   Great influencers: prepare, listen, are flexible, ask rather than tell, are fascinated by people, want agreements to stick, learn, write notes, ask for feedback and never consider themselves an expert.

How did it go?

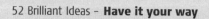

42

It's not just what you say ...

We all intuitively know that there's more to communication than just the words. Great influencers use eye contact, facial expressions and posture to back up what they say.

This is known also as body language, or more formally non-verbal communication (NVC). How we use it can help or hinder our overall communication.

Have you ever been in a discussion with someone, trying to resolve an issue, working hard at influencing, and they never smile? Makes you feel uncomfortable, doesn't it? Or did they sit there, leaning back with folded arms? Infuriating, isn't it? Or when they talked to you did they use their pen to point at you? Rude, isn't it? You have experienced body language at its worst. It might be deliberate; it might be unconscious. Either way it is not helping the discussion.

On the other hand, occasional smiles at appropriate times can make the whole discussion seem more amicable, even if at the moment there doesn't seem to be much common ground. Turning to face the person and keeping arms and hands open just seems more welcoming, as do slower, gentler gestures.

Here's an idea for you...

At your next influencing situation, think as much about your non-verbal communication as you do your verbal and do two things. First, choose NVC that reinforces your message (e.g. open palms to show you are open and listening rather than clenched fists). Second, ensure your NVC is in line with your verbal communication (e.g. your movements are slow – rather than fast and punctuated – to match your slower, considerate voice).

The bottom-line message is: whatever you say verbally will be reinforced by appropriate body language or weakened by the wrong kind.

Here's what will help:

- *Smiling.* This indicates a willingness to work together.
- *Open gestures* (e.g. open palm). This indicates an openness to ideas.
- *Eye contact.* This says I'm listening; I'm attentive.
- *Turning 'square on' to fully face the person.* This reinforces your willingness to reach an agreement.
- *Slower gestures.* This indicates that something is considered important.

Here's what will probably hinder:

- *No expression, or frowns.* This may indicate: I don't like you and/or the idea/s.
- *Pointing.* This may indicate a 'you and me' feeling rather than 'us'.
- *Avoiding eye contact/always looking at notes or laptop.* This says: I'm not interested in your views.
- *Sitting at an angle when talking.* Says: I'm deliberately keeping 'separate' from your ideas.
- *Punctuated gestures.* Indicates impatience: let's just get this done.

Try this exercise. For each of the following situations, state the worst and best NVC. Don't think about it; do it. Don't read ahead until you have done all of them.

1. Sitting in the head teacher's office waiting for her to return so you can discuss your daughter's apparent repeated wearing of a too-short skirt.

2. Speaking on the phone with the bank, who have charged you a massive unauthorised overdraft fee.

3. Walking up to the girl in accounts who you get on really well with and asking her if she would like to go out for a meal with you.

How did you do? In situation 1, helpful NVC would be to stand as she returns (not out of respect, out of confidence) and greet her with a firm hand-shake; smile; sit, ideally to the side of the desk, and maintain good eye contact. It would hinder to stay seated with a hunched posture (suggesting you're passive/fearful); or sit with arms folded and point (suggesting aggression). Sitting 'perched' on the desk would make you appear intimidating.

In situation 2, it helps to stand, and walk around if you can. Look up. Feel good and in control. It hinders to sit in a hunched position and remain still. That way, you feel vulnerable. For situation 3, walk slowly and steadily up to the girl. Keep good eye contact and smile. Ask clearly and gaily, then pause and wait for her response. Don't shuffle up to her, avoiding eye contact or staring at the floor. Don't stand to one side of her. Don't speak quickly with a tone that sounds like you expect her to say 'no'.

'I speak two languages: body and English.'
MAE WEST

Defining idea...

Q **What about reading the body language of others so that you have an advantage over them?**

A *Perhaps you could but be careful here not to take it too far. Body language is not an absolute science. If someone has their arms folded, they may be defensive but also they may simply be feeling chilly! So, do look for all the clues before jumping to a conclusion. Having said that, proper observation of the person you are attempting to influence will certainly help with some fundamentals such as: Are they buying into this idea or not? Did they like that particular suggestion or not? Are they really listening or not?*

Q **What about eye movements themselves? I have heard you can tell whether people are lying simply from the way they move their eyes.**

A *There is certainly some truth in this but, again, don't take it as an 'absolute'. Essentially, if you are looking directly at someone and their eyes move to your right, then they are recalling something (e.g. a previous agreement). If their eyes go left, they are 'constructing'. How might that be useful? Let's imagine you are discussing with your new landlord about whether all problems in the past with earlier tenants have been sorted to his tenants' satisfaction, a recall eye movement may be more reassuring to you than a construct movement.*

43

Keep it private: be loyal

Don't talk about your problems and plans to those who are not involved, or not without a great deal of thought. You never know who else will get to hear them.

Influencing, especially on something sensitive such as salary or a relationship issue, could be weakened if others get to hear your thoughts before you are ready to express them in full.

Stay loyal. Stay private. Stay confidential. And don't confuse this with the valid process of 'talking things through'. Your boss is not very keen on your job-share idea anyway, and then he overhears a couple of people talking about it in the canteen, about apparently how you have 'forced the management' into doing it. Of course, that's probably not the way you shared it – but you know what Chinese whispers are like. You can imagine how annoyed your boss is.

You and your girlfriend have put aside this Saturday to try to get to the bottom of what's currently going wrong in your relationship and then you get an e-mail from one of her friends making some suggestions. You know the friend probably means well, but you feel irritated that she has clearly been told some intimate details about you that, to be honest, you feel should strictly be between just you and your girlfriend.

Here's an idea for you... **Experiment for one week in being totally loyal. No gossip and never say anything negative about someone behind their back. Never reveal any details of planned influencing that you know deep-down you ought not to: prices/rents/salary/company information/partner details. There's a good chance you'll find it refreshing. And it will take you a step further towards being a brilliant influencer, too.**

Never, ever divulge any details of any influencing you are doing unless you do definitely need third-party advice and the person you talk to is scrupulously loyal. Otherwise it may well weaken your case, or worse.

Here are some useful deflection phrases:

- Thanks, but we are not ready to talk to others about it yet.
- It's kind of you to help, but the details are still confidential.
- This is one thing I do need to sort out on my own.
- It would not be fair on them if I were to reveal what they have offered.
- Absolutely: in a week or two your offer of 'talking it through' may be very helpful.
- It's just the way we like to work.

So, what would you do in the following situations?

1. A colleague comes up to you and says he's having a lot of problems with a mutual colleague. He asks if he can talk it through with you.

2. You are in a wine bar and a girlfriend of yours asks, 'How's it going patching up things with your boyfriend?'

3. You are trying to negotiate with HR at your company for a crèche. It's very delicate at the moment and colleagues keep asking you for progress reports.

4. You've spotted a flat being sold privately and you know it's an excellent price. Friends keep asking you how you're getting along with the flat-hunting.

In situation 1, you say: 'Of course.' But check first whether it might be a breach of any other loyalties you have. If so, politely refuse. If not, then only discuss facts and don't get sucked into character assassinations.

Your relationship is actually terrible at the moment and although both you and your boyfriend claim to want it to work, it's at a very tricky stage. So in situation 2 you say: 'It's very difficult at the moment; that's why I'm not talking about it.' And then don't talk about it.

When you're in situation 3 you need to think how not to compromise your negotiations. Be honest and say that it would be unfair on the company to reveal all the details at the moment because they have asked you not to in case it raises hopes too quickly.

Situation 4 requires a little caution. It sounds like your friends are only showing a polite interest so say, 'Overall, great.' But don't reveal the details of this great bit of influencing you are doing with the private seller until the flat's definitely yours. You never know who knows who.

'Loyalty means nothing unless it has at its heart the principle of self-sacrifice.'
WOODROW WILSON

Defining idea…

How did
it go?

Q **But won't my friends feel hurt later on when they hear what's going on and they find out it's been happening for two months?**

A *Possibly. But what's the bigger picture here? It's that you need to sort out this relationship for good. You know your boyfriend hates it when you tell endless stories about him to your girlfriends behind his back, so why not for the moment respect that? It'll make sure you have a better chance of influencing him as you try to work things out.*

Q **Chatting it through with someone is really helpful so why are you saying I shouldn't do that?**

A *Okay, sometimes talking things through can help. For instance, when: you get a different view; you get sympathy at a difficult time; someone reminds you that you may be rationalising too much; someone encourages you to stop talking and to actually do something. On the other hand, it doesn't help when talking it through becomes gossiping, a 'bitching' session, or a time 'to plot'. That can be downright dangerous.*

44

Stuck? Then try something new

'I can't get him to change, no matter what I do. I seem to need help.' Perhaps not: maybe you just need to change what you're doing or the way you're doing it.

There are so many things we want to change — the local council's stupid refuse policy, for one — but they seem so far beyond us that we can begin to think we have no influence at all.

You badly wish to influence, on a daily basis: your son's room tidying habits (lack of); world peace (more, please); your neighbour's inconsiderate car parking (what about your cars?); your girlfriend's smoking (no, please stop). But, after trying for so long, some of them seem so impossible to tackle that you feel like giving up.

Now, stop that! Take a break and have a breather. Step back and admit to yourself you've got into a rut and your current approach probably isn't ever going to work. Your persistence might be admirable, but it's probably gone beyond that – you're into an unhelpful pattern. So, you ask: what is a pattern?

Here's an idea for you... **Take any daily habit. Your route to work, the time you get up. The cereal you eat, the time you check your e-mail. Break them! Take a different route to work. Eat a different cereal ... It's fun isn't it? Break a few more! It's small stuff, agreed. But, by doing this, you have just got better at breaking patterns and that will make you a better influencer.**

- You're keeping on shouting.
- You're keeping on leaving sarcastic notes on his desk.
- You're keeping on ringing the same person at the council.
- You're keeping on sitting in the canteen and complaining about 'the management' to everybody who will listen.
- You're keeping on buying books on how to give up smoking but they never get read.
- You're keeping on using the same PowerPoint deck to try to sell to the customers.

Notice a common word there? Yep, you're doing things the same old way. Now you know what a pattern is. Next you need to work on breaking those patterns.

Did you know that the human brain is naturally pattern-seeking? (Stick with this; it is interesting and relevant.) It's known as an 'evolutionary double-bind', which is both good news and bad news. The good news is that we spot patterns very easily: doors, faces, strategies. We don't need to learn every new one each time; we can generalise. The bad news is that we often choose the same old pattern time after time after time: same route to work (despite it being choked with traffic), same shouting at the kids (despite it never working).

These patterns are designed for our safety: that's why we easily recognise a face with just a few clues. And patterns make our lives easier: they're a sort of shorthand so that we don't have to start every process from scratch. So, of course they are not all bad! But they can hinder our ability to have it our way. Breaking patterns can get results.

All very well, you say, but how do we do that? To start with, when you get a result you don't want, ask yourself what pattern might have led to this result. You'll notice it is often an unhelpful one. And then break it by doing something different.

- Instead of keeping on shouting, try talking softly and with tenderness.
- Instead of keeping on leaving sarcastic notes on his desk, try walking up to him and discussing your point over a coffee.
- Instead of keeping on ringing the same person at the council, try their boss or your MP.
- Instead of keeping on sitting in the canteen complaining about 'the management', try writing a 'proposal for positive change' and circulating it.
- Instead of keeping on buying quit-smoking books that are never read, book a session with a hypnotherapist.
- Instead of keeping using the same PowerPoint deck to sell to the customers, tell some great stories about client successes.

'If you keep doing the same thing, you'll keep getting the same result.'
PHIL STAMP, theoretical physicist

Defining idea...

189

Breaking a pattern involves some key things:

- Change of thinking (e.g. this redundancy is an opportunity, not a threat).
- Change of body language (e.g. acting as if in control rather than stressed).
- Change of voice (e.g. soft rather than harsh).

There are other subtle things that will all help you become more of a pattern breaker. Read more widely and outside your main area. Spend time with new and different people. Travel. Watch yourself and ask: 'what does this say about me?'

Remember to give it time: the patterns you've adopted have often developed over a life-time. If you can slow down a little, you'll be better able to 'notice' where your own patterns are entrenched. And pay attention to feedback, especially on your own poor behaviour, because this can often highlight the symptoms of poor patterns.

Q But isn't persistence important?

A Yes, it's excellent, but if it's still not working after a good dose of persistence it's time to move on. One tip when trying to influence is the rule of three: try the same approach three times. If it fails to work, try another approach and then try that three times, etc. You are then getting the benefit of persistence and flexibility. Persistence is a pattern and it is generally seen as a positive one but, of course, when it shifts into an obsession, then it becomes less helpful.

Q How do I actually break a pattern?

A When you spot the pattern, do parts of it differently. For instance, take a break at a different time; write instead of phone; read for inspiration and talk to someone new about the problem; leave the problem on the back-burner for a whole week; talk about it on a walk rather than the office; instead of asking them to give up smoking, ask them to work on their health; use Wikipedia rather than your usual source; use another source rather than your usual Wikipedia. You get the picture.

How did it go?

45

Have it your way by being flexible

Great influencing is about being flexible. And that's you, right? You do see that there's more than one way to get the result you're after. And that's why you'll get it.

There are many ways for you to raise the capital for your start-up. Consider them all. There are many ways your teenager could 'put things right'. Consider them all.

Any of these situations require influencing if you are going to get your own way:

- You want a salary increase.
- You need to live back at your parents' home after university, but you don't want to pay rent.
- You think it would be better for your young children if you moved to the country but your wife isn't keen: she says it would be too quiet.

And 'your way' is presumably: more money/a room but no rent/a move to the country. And, more than that, you'll probably have a specific way you want 'your

Here's an idea for you... **With the next influencing situation you go into, keep in mind the 'big picture' and look for the issues on which your flexibility will give you an edge. Say you're looking for a discount on a new car. Do you care that the number plate will make it appear not to be this year's model when you know it'll still be in truth brand new? Then negotiate with the sales people when they're desperate to shift their current stock to boost their annual results. The more you try this, the more creative you'll become.**

way' to be: 4.5% a.s.a.p./no more hassle on the rent issue/the house going up for sale and looking at properties in the countryside.

But what about looking at it with a broader agenda? Try getting a clearer view of what you actually want:

■ Do you actually want to be better off in money terms *or* do you want a better 'measure' of your worth?

■ You actually want to start saving to get your own place, so cash is important to you.

■ You're actually worried about the social problems in the local environment.

To think outside the box, you need to know what the box is; you need to have a handle on what is desirable, what is key, what is essential. Once you know what the box really is, you can become more flexible. And when you're flexible, you increase your chances of being successful. Thus:

■ If you want to be better off and feel more valued, maybe your employer could help with a travel season ticket loan or a different pension plan.

■ If you want to hang on to cash, fine, but maybe there's a whole range of chores you could agree with your parents that would ensure they feel valued too.

■ And do you need to move to the country to achieve this? What about a different location in your current city? Sure, it's more expensive, but you'll also be adding a lot of ongoing expenses when you move out to the country.

Before you go into any influencing situation, agree with yourself that you will increase your chances of being more flexible by spending some time getting very clear on what it is you really want.

■ A new relationship, or most of the current one with a few changes?
■ More money in this job or to be valued?
■ To move house or just to revitalise the current home environment?
■ To lose weight or to have more energy?

How do you boost that flexibility? One way is to be more curious about the other options. Ask yourself questions such as:

■ If there were a different way of doing this, what would it be?
■ What would happen if we didn't reach any agreement?
■ What would happen if I delayed?
■ If Richard Branson had a suggestion, what would he say?

'The map is not the territory.'
ALFRED KORZYBSKI, originator of semantics

Defining idea...

You should also force yourself to write a list of different ways to achieve the same end. Go on a long walk and as soon as you get back, grab a pen and write down any new ideas that have surfaced. Ask a trusted person to play devil's advocate with you. Do an online search on the topic and see where it leads you.

In summary: to think outside the box, to be flexible, you need to know what the box is. You need to know what you are really after.

Q **Isn't being flexible a sign of being a pushover?**

A *Possibly, but you know you aren't and that's what's important. When you have thought through all the options that will still fundamentally give you what you want, you are in fact being very strong. You'll find that win–win situation that leaves you in the driving seat. And when you repeatedly 'get it your way' through thinking differently, that will be noticeable to others, too.*

Q **I'm comfortable with being flexible but how do I get *them* to be flexible as well?**

A *Here's a story you might like. One day a mother and her son came up to Gandhi in the market place. The mother asked Gandhi if he could tell her son to give up sugar. Gandhi thought for a while and then said: 'Yes, come back in a week and I will do it.' The mother was surprised why Gandhi couldn't just do it there and then, but she was at least pleased that he would do it. In a week's time, she met Gandhi and he turned to her son and said: 'You must give up sugar because it is not good for your health.' The boy did so. Later, the mother was very appreciative and asked Gandhi why he hadn't been able to say that when they first met. He replied: 'I needed to give up sugar myself, first.' The message is that you need to be the change you want to see in others. Be flexible and they will become more flexible.*

How did it go?

197

46

Keep a journal

Capturing life's ups and downs in a journal is amazingly therapeutic and often shows you either a better way to influence or the issues that are usually best forgotten.

The act of writing down what has been going on in your days is an ideal way to reflect on the minutiae you might have missed at the time it happened and learn important lessons.

Stuff happens, doesn't it? There's a reorganisation at your company and at a stroke your career path appears over. You bump into an old school friend and she is now running her own PR company and needs someone to head up events and she invites you. Plus a 15% increase in salary. You spot your boyfriend in a bar in animated conversation with an attractive girl. You say nothing and go home fuming. Within twelve hours you find out it was his sister, and she works at the new company you will be joining.

Here's an idea for you...

Spend some time writing every day for fifteen days. Whether you think it is useful or not, just try it. At the end of fifteen days you will be a better influencer. Here are some tips to help you. Just write: don't wait until you are in the mood. If in doubt, simply describe any situation: you will find your feelings and self observations will appear readily enough. If you get stuck, simply say 'and'. Aim at writing a couple of A4 pages every day, whatever your mood.

Such things go on every day and a lot of it needs managing using the best of your influencing skills. But does it need to be tackled immediately? Not always. And sometimes it's worth just letting things go – the career that wasn't really happening; the relationship that had run its course. Not everything has to be fixed, influenced, made perfect.

And that's where your journal will really help; it'll make you a better influencer and a whole lot better at getting the right things your way. So, how's it done?

Firstly, you need the equipment. Go to the best stationery shop you can find and examine with care all the notebooks you can see: brand-name ones; cheap ones; expensive ones; small and large ones. There are a few key things to consider. What size works for you? If the page size is too small, you'll find your 'flow' is cramped. Check the paper surface: will it work with the pen you plan to use, especially if you like a fountain pen or a pencil? Different writing implements prefer different surfaces. If necessary stock up on pens or ink cartridges or whatever you need.

Secondly, you need to establish a routine. Write every day and if possible in the same place (e.g. at your desk) and at the same time. That rigid routine will make it easier for you to stick to it.

Thirdly, just write. Start with the influencing scenario. How can I get my boyfriend to take us having children seriously? What can I do to influence my father to give up driving now that he is 83? What would convince the board to give me the vacant HR position? And then just write.

Finally, look back on your work, but never immediately: leave it twenty-four hours, or a week or even a month. The passage of time will have allowed reflection and perspective. Couple these and you get great learning.

Look at journal entries from a year ago and you should be able to see how well your influencing has matured. To kick-start your reflection, you may well like to consider these questions as you read back through the pages:

- When do I influence well?
- What makes me a poor influencer?
- Do I seem to have some approaches I could develop more?
- What are my weak points and which other brilliant ideas could help?
- Are there any cases of influencing where I now look back and realise I could have done it better? In what way/s?
- What seemed important at the time, but much less so now?
- Which have been my really great influencing successes?

Defining idea…

'*Retreating in a New Mexico hideaway at the time, Julia Cameron knew there must be a way to find out what she should and could be doing with her talents. She began writing a few pages every day into a journal, and soon discovered characters and plots evolving from those pages.*'
ELEANOR SULLO, author and poet

How did it go?

Q **I do like the idea of a journal, but I've tried it twice and given up. How could I make it work for me?**

A   We could be rude and tell you simply to try again, but that probably wouldn't be helpful. Well, do try again but this time accept that it often takes time to get into the process so stick with it. Writing about your influencing experiences provides precisely the clear focus you might need to get started and stick at it. It gives you a clear goal.

Q **I'd love to have a journal, but my writing is so bad that even I can't always read it. What can I do?**

A   If you can put pen to paper, that's all you need. Don't worry about quality of writing as nobody is reading it apart from you. Our goal is not to produce literature, but to provide an opportunity for learning. So, it's all going to be fine – just get pen and paper and start.

Q **I know you won't be pleased me asking this, but aren't journals a girlie thing?**

A   Some journal writing is definitely preferred by girls/ladies, especially when it's about relationships. But we are not really doing that here: we're looking at the bigger picture of influencing scenarios. So, get on with it and don't tell anyone about it if it concerns you! If you're a bloke, well, call it scenario planning. Just get on with it for goodness sake! Men!

47

Discuss what will help, not what won't

When influencing, think hard about whether and how much to go over old ground. Focus on what can change, which is of course the future not the past.

History is sometimes, well, just history — it won't happen again. Yes, you can draw lessons from the past, but great influencing is usually a forward-looking process.

Get one thing clear. Are we influencing because there is something we don't like and if we get it sorted it will help us and maybe others in the future? Well, that sounds great. Or are we influencing because there is something we don't like and we want retribution – we want pay-back? Hmm, that doesn't sound so good.

Examples of the former (i.e. positive influencing) would include influencing someone to achieve:

- Better child-care arrangements.
- A sensible salary for the unsociable hours you do.
- A better arrangement about who gets called out if the office alarm goes off.

Here's an idea for you... **On any occasion when you are considering doing some influencing ask these questions: Will this still be important in 30 minutes? (The person who bumped into you on the tube: *no*, so don't bother.) Will this still be important tomorrow? (The way you were spoken to by the head of geography at the parents' evening: *yes*, so start influencing.) Will this still be important in one year? (The way your boyfriend talks about you to his office friends: *absolutely*, so start influencing.)**

- A working arrangement for who goes where at Christmas time.
- A decent deal with your accountant about the VAT mistake.
- They pay for your dress to be dry-cleaned after spilling sauce down the back of it.

Examples of the latter (i.e. negative, no-point-to-it influencing) would be influencing someone because:

- You didn't like the way they spoke to you (but you will never have to see them again).
- They talked behind your back (but they are leaving your office anyway).

And even if it is worth influencing – as in the positive cases – still concentrate on what is relevant and what is not relevant.

Of course, the same principle should be stressed when someone is trying to influence you and they keep referring to irrelevant past events. Remind them if that is so with phrases such as:

- I know and I've already apologised for that; it will not happen again.
- But that was when we were both very different; it's no longer relevant.
- That was a mistake I made which I won't make again.
- Please don't refer to that project – it was a one-off, as you know. It has no bearing on this team.

You might like this story to get you thinking. Two monks lived in a monastery. Here, everyone had taken a vow of silence. One day the monks were summoned to the head monk's office and asked to deliver, by hand, an important letter to another monastery some 25 km away. The monks set off, in silence of course, as they had been for the past eight years. After walking for hours they came to a river; the water was flowing high and fast. On the bank there was a beautiful girl and she was crying.

The monks looked at each other and then the slightly taller one said to the girl: 'This will be brief as I have a vow of silence: what is the problem?' The girl explained that there was meant to be a ferryman but she'd been here all day and there was no sign of him and she had to get to her sick aunt's house, which was not far but was on the other side of the river.

The tall monk said: 'Jump on my shoulders and we will wade across. My fellow monk will help me stay stable.' And so the girl jumped on his shoulder and hung on tight. The other monk looked distressed but helped them wade across. It was tough but they did it. The girl thanked them profusely. Neither monk said anything; the taller monk smiled and they carried on their way.

A couple of hours later, just as the sun was setting and they were approaching their destination, the slightly shorter monk burst out: 'I cannot believe you did that. Not only did you talk, but you touched a very desirable girl.'

The slightly taller monk replied: 'Brother, I let down my baggage at the waterside. I think you still need to let go of yours.'

> '*History will be kind to me for I intend to write it.*'
> WINSTON CHURCHILL

Defining
idea...

How did it go?

Q But – dare I say it – isn't it okay to get revenge, especially when someone deserves it?

A *By all means let someone know they've done you a disservice, or how you feel about them. However, don't try and change them if you are not going to be involved with them again. Revenge often does feel good at the time, but most of us admit it tends to leave a 'bitter-sweet taste' afterwards. Save your energy for more important causes.*

Q Should you always influence when it could have a future impact?

A *We would strongly suggest yes. You see, if you let something go – e.g. the person talking during your presentation; your boss not doing your management review; the newspaper shop delivering your paper late – and you don't influence, you are really saying that that behaviour is acceptable; do it again in the future. And that, of course, is not what you want. So: tackle it. It may well seem hard at the time, but think how much hassle it will save you in the future.*

48

Live and let live

Is it really worth it? Has it become too much a matter of principle? Or, worse, obsession? Could you swallow your pride, let it go and be happier in the long term?

All of us will sometimes arrive at the point when we just need to realise enough is enough.

The neighbours and the overhanging tree; your boyfriend and the towels dropped on the floor; your son's school and silly uniform regulations; HR and their poxy forms. Every single one of them drives you mad, but is it worth fighting the battle to change them and have it your way?

The answer is 'yes' if:

- ... it'll have a big positive impact to your future (e.g. it'll stop all future silly form-filling),
- ... it's a principle and an important one (e.g. the school said the expensive uniform was compulsory but now you have found that not all parents follow the code).

Here's an idea for you...

When an influencing challenge looms and you know you're going to have to put some energy in, ask yourself some questions. Will this matter in a few weeks or months? If so: get to work. If not: forget it. What about the relationships involved? If you can cope with any fall-out, get to work. And if the first and second answers contradict each other (e.g. it is an important issue but it could damage the relationship), ask a supplementary question: can you live with a lost principle because of persevering with an important relationship? Then you'll know if it's worth pressing ahead, all guns blazing.

But it'll be a 'no' if:

- ... it damages relationships and you gain little (e.g. the tree only overhangs your garden by a couple of feet and it'd be a shame to fall out with your long-standing neighbours),
- ... it's just a quirk of yours (e.g. your boyfriend is great and actually quite tidy, so you can cope with those dropped towels – after all, there's a fair number of your poor habits with which he has to cope). Few of us are perfect!

Here's a story you might like to think about.

A jogger was running along the beach on a glorious morning. He did this every morning as a way to keep fit but also to give him some thinking time to reflect on his work and home life.

Suddenly, as he rounded the headland, he was horrified to see the beautiful sand ahead looked stained. Initially, he thought it was an oil-slick but as he got close he saw it was countless starfish, trapped by the tide going out. And amongst them was a young boy who was picking them up and hurling them back out to sea.

The runner called out to the boy: 'You can't save them; there's too many.' But the boy ignored him. Standing next to the boy, the jogger repeated his message: 'There's no point; you can't save them all.' But the boy continued. As he hurled another starfish back into the sea, he said: 'There's a lot of point for this one. And this one. And this one.'

The jogger shook his head and ran on. But then he stopped and turned around. For the rest of the morning he worked hard to assist the boy in his efforts.

So, how do we decide when enough is enough? There are points that we all reach when we should admit that the time has come to let it drop:

- When we can no longer remember what the battle is about.
- When really strong emotions – such as 'hate' – are being expressed.
- When a good friend suggests that maybe we have got things way out of proportion.
- When it is taking up a huge amount of our time.

And how do we then cope with letting it go?

- Put it down to helping our development.
- Use it as a great learning experience that will make us better influencers.
- Look on it as a sign of our maturity that we can 'let it go'.

'Ring the bells that still can ring / Forget your perfect offering / There is a crack in everything / That's how the light gets in.'
LEONARD COHEN

Defining idea...

After you have let go, occupy your mind with something else: good friends, go for a walk to clear your mind, reading and music. Then you'll be ready to get back to what you used to do and tackle other – more important – issues!

Q **Surely there's a right and a wrong to every situation and it should be talked through according to those rules? And if they are wrong, you should get it sorted.**

A *If only it were that simple. You know your father is sometimes rude to your children, but after all he's nearly 90. So rather than try and influence him and possibly lose the relationship you'd rather teach the children the essential skill of working with older people. You know the corner shop is often very unreliable with their paper delivery but for the moment you'd rather support them in the fight against the big supermarket. You can always get the main news online until it arrives.*

Q **What about if somebody accuses you of worrying too much and not being willing to let something go – but you actually do think it is important? You do want to have it your way.**

A *Step back and take a moment or two to think: could they be right? Has this moved from something important to a passion to an obsession? Take the feedback, think about it and possibly, move on. If you still feel – all things considered – that it remains an issue, then fight on and ignore the snide comments.*

49

Summarise (and agree)

Your memory is not perfect; nor is theirs. Misunderstandings occur. So, write notes as you go. Keep summarising. Keep agreeing. Do you understand each other properly?

Perhaps you could drop them an e-mail to confirm. Whatever, stay close and keep in touch. It's all worth it to get what you want and to ensure you have it your way.

It's pretty exciting when you've been doing some influencing and believe you've reached an agreement on the colour (pale chocolate) of the new bathroom with your sister, or you've been let off the parking fine after a lengthy telephone discussion with the council, or you've been excused the Saturday shift because of the wedding you need to attend.

However, it's pretty frustrating when you find that the apparent agreement unravels. Your sister mentions to your mother that she thought banana would be a great colour, after all; the full parking fine turns up in the post anyway; and you get an angry voice-mail from your boss on the way to the wedding, saying: where the bl**dy h*ll are you?

Here's an idea for you...

You know you love those courtroom dramas: 'I rest my case, m'lud' etc. Try imagining your little bit of influencing has to be robust enough to survive a cross-examination. Not just where were you on the night of the 12th, not just how come your shoe matches the footprint in the flower bed, but all the way down to the DNA testing. Yes, that rigorous. If you manage to pick some holes in your case, so will the person you are trying to influence and you'll be thrown out of court.

Here's a brilliant idea to help – and, as always, it's nice and simple. Summarise, and summarise a lot. Summarise verbally. Summarise in writing. It'll ensure you get none of the problems we mentioned above.

We summarise and agree for three main reasons. The first is to check our and their understanding. By reviewing all of the points and then asking 'do you agree?' we can ensure we both of us believe in the same points and are therefore highly likely to act upon them. The second is a more tactical point: summarising pulls the discussion/meeting right back to the main discussion points, so it is an excellent approach if minds are wandering. And the third, of course, is to get a great return on all the good work we have put into these discussions so far. For example:

With your sister

Not: Yep, I think chocolate would be good, too.

Try: Chocolate would be good. Here's the colour card. Are you happy with that before I buy the cans of paint? Do we need to check with Mum? Thought so. Well, you've got until 4.00 then I'm off to the paint shop. I'll catch you later for a final decision.

On the phone re the parking ticket

Not: Great – I'm glad we could resolve this.

Try: Mr Smith, you've been very helpful. Obviously you'll want confirmation in
writing, what's your e-mail address? Perfect. I'll drop you an e-mail as soon as
I put the phone down, then we both know exactly where we are. Thank you
so much for your help.

With your shift supervisor

Not: Cool. My friend will be so pleased that I've got the time off to go to her
wedding.

Try: Who do I need to get a decision from in HR? I know it's not always necessary,
but I really wouldn't want to let my friend down.

Here are some practical tips for the 'summarise and agree' process:

- Look them in the eye and make good eye contact as you ask for agreement. Do
their eyes flicker? Hmm … worrying sign!
- Shut up: don't give them the answer! Ask for their agreement and pause until
they give it.
- Get confirmation: a yes, a no, whatever: get
it in the positive.
- Use bullet-points to summarise what you
are agreeing in a nice, easy list.

**Mitch McDeere: 'Are you
saying my life is in danger?'
Denton Voyles: 'I am saying
your life as you know it is
over.'**
JOHN GRISHAM, *The Firm*

*Defining
idea…*

213

- Double-check: there's no harm in asking twice if you are a little concerned.
- Put it in writing and be explicit. It should leave no doubt at all: not just 'the price we agreed', but '500 euros, as agreed'.
- Get a date: when will this happen?
- Ask 'is there anything else?' Ask 'are you happy with that?' Check nothing can hold up the agreement.
- Check detail: so can you get it in red?
- Ask for their name and position (so, Mr Bloggs, you are able to agree this, is that right?) and confirm accountability (will it be you who ensures this is sorted out?).
- Write down what they say – as they say it. This always focuses someone's mind.

Q **I hate precision. What's wrong with my usual laid back approach?**

How did it go?

A *I know: but you hate agreements which unravel even more, don't you? You see, you will have done an awful lot of work so far; why throw it all away? Why not tie the string on the parcel? Why not light the candles on the cake? That's all it's about. It's no big deal. Look them in the eyes and check all is as you expected. Send them an e-mail confirming everything. Just a couple of key questions – and waiting for good answers – is all it takes. It'll save you a lot of stress later on. Really.*

Q **What about if there is nobody I can pin down for that final agreement?**

A *There always is; you need to look harder, look further. Ask for their manager or team-leader in the shop. Ask for who runs that department at the council. Ask for the name of the bank's area manager. There is always someone. And if there really isn't anyone you can pin down, you may have an agreement that's going to unravel very quickly.*

50

Be polite and be persistent

Whatever happens, if you can maintain a decent relationship with the person you want to influence, that'll give you the best chance of having it your way in the end.

If you're rude to people, they're not likely to give you the time of day. That's why you should be polite and be persistent. It is a winning formula every time.

- It's ridiculous! The salesman said you would get 500 free texts on your phone, but your bill shows you have not had that allowance. Trying to get some sense out of these people is like pulling teeth ... and the number of people you have spoken to ... *But*, should you have shouted at that last guy who finally answered your call and asked your password again?
- She's only your daughter's drama teacher, after all. Who does she think she is saying your daughter has very little talent for acting? *But*, should you have walked off in a huff?
- That's an outrage! The house will cost you three-quarters of a million pounds and they want you to pay hundreds of pounds extra for their curtains ... *But*, should you have told the agents to stick the deal where the sun don't shine if they're going to be like that?
- And the bank ... they spend millions, you presume, convincing you to borrow money. You then do, the economy gets a bit tight and they're over you like a rash ... *But*, was it a good idea to be rude to that 'idiot' assistant manager?

Here's a quest for you for the coming week: strengthen the emotional bank account you have with the main person you are currently influencing. Make deposits in the usual way – do what you promise, be supportive, be on time, be respectful and listen to really understand – but then put a cherry on the cake. Be ever so, ever so nice. Be helpful (this does not mean weak; just helpful). Be charming. Notice how it is totally disarming and very profitable in having it your way.

Yes, doing what you did was understandable, but it's rarely fair to behave like that. After all, those people are just doing their jobs. And behaving like that rarely gets results – it makes them less likely to help you and simply gives you another stressful day.

So, what's to be done when people let us down, move too slowly, or don't enable us to get things the way we want? Well, don't let go of that frustrated energy. Harness it and use it in a different way. Channel it into two devastating forces: politeness and persistence. They are world-beating qualities to harness.

So, what does polite mean? Politeness is:

- Not raising your voice.
- Talking to the other person by name. ('So, Tim, how can I get a refund?')
- Not being sarcastic.
- Thanking the other person for every concession, however small. ('Sally, that's brilliant. Thank you.')
- Not threatening them. (You'll get an unproductive reception when you say, 'If you don't sort this, I will report you to your manager.')
- Being reasonable. ('Well, it's not ideal but I guess I will leave it at that.')

Basically, don't attack them; attack the problem. And if you make progress, make sure you acknowledge that step forward by thanking them. Sending a 'thank you' message will make the purr. Send a note to their manager saying how brilliant they were will be the cherry on the cake.

What does persistent mean? Persistence is:

- Keeping on asking for what is rightfully yours. ('Actually, Vip, as we agreed, I do want that corrected in writing.')
- Looking for that one someone who can help. ('Do you think your team leader could help?')
- Not taking 'no' for an answer. ('I'd like someone who could give me a proper answer to ring me back.')
- Keeping on writing and leaving messages.
- Keeping on trying but also keeping on trying in different ways.

Work with the other person's emotional bank account. Do the same as you would to keep the manager of your financial bank account happy. She likes it if you make regular deposits if you are going to make regular withdrawals (and more deposits than withdrawals!), and that you chat to her very carefully before making any unauthorised withdrawals.

Being rude is one such withdrawal but there are many others that can take you into the red. Avoid:

> '**True politeness is perfect ease and freedom. It simply consists of treating others just as you love to be treated yourself.'**
> 4th EARL OF CHESTERFIELD

Defining idea…

- Letting someone down
- Talking behind their back, negatively
- Being late and disorganised
- Making assumptions
- Judging before knowing/understanding.

Q   **Being polite all the time makes me feel like I'm being servile. What's wrong with a bit of hard-ball assertiveness?**

A   *Some people do initially think that being polite makes us look weak. That's because, unfortunately, aggression has become so strongly associated with strength. Bear in mind that when you are polite and persistent you should always be able to keep the relationship intact. That is important for the higher reason of treating people decently and also the more pragmatic reason of you never know when you might meet that person again and need their support. So, politeness is strength. It's a powerful boost to assertiveness, too.*

Q   **Aren't there any occasions when 'losing it' can help?**

A   *Yes. There is no doubt that if you are generally polite, fair and persistent, and then you suddenly raise your volume, that will have a dramatic effect on people, which could lead to you rapidly getting what you want. But it may backfire and it can only be done once. So think very, very carefully before you use this powerful secret weapon. Avoid justifying it by saying 'it was the only way I could knock some sense into him'. With a bit of consideration, there's generally a better way and, of course, although we do want to have it our way, we do want to maintain the relationship.*

51

Be sensitive to 'buy-in' signals

You can stop banging on now – you've influenced them; you're going to have it your way. Save your energy: learn to recognise signals of success and know when to stop.

You're on a roll. You give them another reason. And another. But if you'd just give them a moment, you'd see they've actually agreed to give you your money back.

It's the big interview and it's been a long time coming. This is the third interview: you've been up most of the night worrying about it, finalising your thoughts, flicking through books to get ideas about how you can secure the best possible financial package. You're invited into the board room and, after a couple of pleasantries, they say: 'And when can you start?' Then you say: 'Well, first of all, I would like to talk about ...' NO: that's an insensitive move.

So you're fuming. You went away for a 'hen' weekend with the girls. When you left, the flat was spotless, and 90% of that effort had been yours. You've walked in and you're close to tears with the mess – the stack of empty beer cans in an overflowing

Here's an idea for you... **Whenever you're in a conversation with someone – at the office, at home, in a shop – look for signs that show that they are 'buying in' to your ideas (a nod, a movement towards you, a question about the detail ...). These are 'buying' signals and show you are making an impression on them. They are the signals you should look for to tell you your influencing is working and you will indeed ensure you have it your way.**

carrier bag by the door; the remnants of take-away curries. And the smell in the flat. He's texted you to say he's on his way home. In he walks, looking smart and carrying a big bunch of flowers. You yell at him: 'If you think those are going to make a difference ...' NO: an insensitive move.

It's been a tough summer with the neighbours. Their new house extension has caused dirt, dust and noise and you have been close to a row on several occasions. Then you get a hand-written card under the door: 'Come to our end-of-summer/new extension barbecue.' You tear it up – 'If they think that's compensation for the anguish we've had ...!' NO: insensitive move.

Be sensitive. Think:

- The bunch of flowers is a positive sign.
- The invite is a positive sign.

Don't turn down a positive sign, even if it is perhaps a simple ploy – as it might be with the bunch of flowers. All positive signs can be used and worked upon. It's important to recognise positive signs because, if we don't, we can actually lose the agreement we were seeking in our keenness to bring all of our argumentation to bear.

When we are influencing, we often put most of our efforts into convincing: into having the best argument, the strongest points, the killer rationale. However, it's even more important that we just listen and notice. How did they respond to that last point? How did they change? Essentially we are looking for any subtle sign that they are buying in to what we are saying. The sign can be verbal (e.g. 'I agree') or non-verbal (e.g. nodding affirmatively).

Here are some examples of verbal positive signs or 'buying signals':

- *Job interview:* How much are you looking for, exactly? How quickly could you start? How quickly could you get us a reference?
- *Relationship issues:* I'm sorry. I hadn't realised. Can we start over? Would you be willing to forget about that?
- *Selling your flat:* Could you tell me about tube lines? Is there a good local pub? Would you be including the curtains?

And some non-verbal ones:

- *Job interview:* Writing figures down on paper.
- *Relationship issues:* Moving close into your space. Smiling.
- *Selling your flat:* Pacing out room dimensions. Contemplatively staring out at the view.

> **'"Why do they buy?" is a thousand times more important than "How do I sell?" No, let me correct that … it's one million times more important than "How do I sell?" No, let me correct that … it's one billion times more important than "How do I sell?" Get the picture?'**
> JEFFREY GITOMER, author

Defining idea…

How did it go?

Q **Shouldn't I give them all the points of my argument? Doesn't that really ensure that they are fully convinced?**

A *No. Sometimes less is more. Yes, we want to have lots of persuasive reasons, and especially if we haven't really reasoned with someone before so we don't necessarily know what works for them. But unravel the points carefully and note the reactions. If you only need one point to get the reaction you want, fantastic! Be aware that firing off too many points can obscure your essential winning argument. Silence is a point: just shut up and see what they say next. They may well need some time to think about your last point.*

Q **Some people don't give much away, though, do they? Especially in a lot of business influencing. What do we do with them? For instance, we've been trying to agree a deal with our architect but you never know what he's thinking.**

A *That's right, some people are just 'low reactors' and don't display much. Some people have been trained not to give away much. And some people are a combination of both. But here's the thing: our reactions do 'leak'. In poker they call it a 'tell'. Small things: they shift their weight; they twiddle their pen; they look out of the window. Just watch a little more closely and listen a little harder. You'll get the clues that you need.*

Remember the dark side

Be positive and be true is our general advice. But sometimes it's worth tapping the 'dark side' as well. Highlighting possible negative outcomes can be effective in influencing.

Good influencing is usually about the good news that comes from the change. However, bad news can be more dramatic: What will happen if you don't revise? What will happen if you don't change your diet?

Think about human nature for a moment: we will do anything for more pleasure and for less pain. That's essentially how our motivations work.

- We have an affair for more pleasure; we never get around to telling our partner in order to avoid pain.
- We eat too much chocolate to gain pleasure; we don't study because of the pain.
- We spend money on clothes because of the pleasure; we don't save because stopping our retail therapy is painful.
- We want the pleasure of being in a band; we don't want the pain of learning the guitar.

Here's an idea for you...

Next time you have some influencing to do, next time you are seeking to have it your way, think 'dark side'. Even if you're a naturally positive person, think: What would be the really bad news on this; what could really build the gloom? Practise really building that gloom, that dark side. Positive side to revision: great grades ... great jobs ... choice ... happy life ... etc. Dark side of no revision: ...pre-exam stress ... weeks of anxiety awaiting results ... poor grades ... embarrassment ... not getting into chosen university ... poor status ... harder to get a job ... harder to develop a decent career ... long-term lack of fulfilment ... life-long unhappiness. Go on, you could lay it on with a trowel!

All human behaviour works on this level. So, if you can harness that fact, then it will help you tremendously with your influencing.

Rather than gaining pleasure, here, we're concerned with avoiding pain – using the 'dark side' to influence. Let's look at some examples to show how it works. We'll start by using what the person we are talking to will gain as a result of agreeing to our (positive) influencing. Then we'll contrast this with the process of dark-side (negative) influencing.

Positive influencing

Example 1: salary. ... if I get a salary increase it will mean that I feel rewarded and much more part of the team. You can expect to see an increase in productivity and a desire to contribute more to the organisation. In addition it will give me a long-term perspective and I will be committed to creating a long-term career here.

Example 2: cleaning the flat. ... if you clean the flat – say, every other week on a shared basis with me – the whole place will be a lot nicer to live in. It will be much more welcoming for our friends and in a way it gets us into some good habits for our planned move to a house.

Example 3: encouraging saving. … if we were to start saving into a special account, we could begin making a plan to buy our first flat. I've seen some calculations on a few websites. With the power of compound interest, it doesn't take much at all.

Example 4: no to the family Christmas. … I just think that if we all agree that none of us have to spend every Christmas together like we did when we were kids, there are two huge benefits. First, anyone who does get together, really does want to, and that should make it less fraught and a lot more fun for everyone. Second, it ensures anyone who wants to do something different at Christmas doesn't feel ostracised by the rest of the family.

Negative – dark-side – influencing

Example 1: salary. … the thing is, if I don't get a salary increase then I will seriously consider leaving and that will mean a significant loss of your investment over the years and an essential player in the team.

Example 2: cleaning the flat. … I'm not sure I can continue to live with someone who has so little respect for his living environment and – to be honest – for me.

Example 3: encouraging saving. … if we don't get saving soon, we'll not have any real security for the rest of our lives.

Example 4: no to the family Christmas. … look, we're all sick of this Christmas pretence. If we don't come to an amicable arrangement for this year, I'm not sure whether any of us will be talking to each other in a year's time.

'Now I'm beginning to wonder. I've been having dreams about the dark side. I want to become a good Jedi and use the powers of the light side, but in my dreams the Emperor and Darth Vader have claimed me for the dark side. What if it is true? What if I can't escape it?'
ANAKIN SKYWALKER, *Star Wars*

Defining idea…

How did
it go?

Q Isn't 'dark side' influencing a bit mean?

A Well, it depends what you mean by 'mean'? Few of us want to hear the problems we could face. We don't want to hear that smoking causes cancer; that not saving reduces our choices; that not hitting our sales quota could lose us our job. However, it does tend to motivate us a little more. So, yes it can be mean, but mean for a very good reason.

Q How 'dark' can I – should I – get?

A Do what it takes to get the job done, assuming the other person has your resources. It would be unreasonable to use 'dark side' influencing to overly cause anxiety in a child, but a teenager does need to understand the dark side of drugs if you are trying to influence them in some positive behaviours when they go out clubbing. And if you can convince your new girlfriend that the positive benefits of cigarettes for her (looking sexy and keeping off the pounds) are not enough to stop cancer, early death, dried-up skin and a mouth which smells like an ash-tray, then do it!

The end...

Or is it a new beginning?

We hope that the ideas in this book will have inspired you to keep a cool head in any situation and taught you a few tricks when it comes to getting what you want. Maybe you've already put some of the tips into practise at work, at home and out in the big wide world.

So why not let us know all about it? Tell us how you got on. What did it for you – what really made you master of your own destiny? Maybe you've got some tips of your own you want to share (see next page if so). And if you liked this book you may find we have even more brilliant ideas that could change other areas of your life for the better.

You'll find the Infinite Ideas crew waiting for you online at www.infideas.com.

Or if you prefer to write, then send your letters to:
Have it your way
The Infinite Ideas Company Ltd
36 St Giles, Oxford OX1 3LD, United Kingdom

We want to know what you think, because we're all working on making our lives better too. Give us your feedback and you could win a copy of another *52 Brilliant Ideas* book of your choice. Or maybe get a crack at writing your own.

Good luck. Be brilliant.

Offer one

CASH IN YOUR IDEAS

We hope you enjoy this book. We hope it inspires, amuses, educates and entertains you. But we don't assume that you're a novice, or that this is the first book that you've bought on the subject. You've got ideas of your own. Maybe our author has missed an idea that you use successfully. If so, why not send it to yourauthormissedatrick@infideas.com, and if we like it we'll post it on our bulletin board. Better still, if your idea makes it into print we'll send you four books of your choice or the cash equivalent. You'll be fully credited so that everyone knows you've had another Brilliant Idea.

Offer two

HOW COULD YOU REFUSE?

Amazing discounts on bulk quantities of Infinite Ideas books are available to corporations, professional associations and other organisations.

For details call us on:
+44 (0)1865 514888
Fax: +44 (0)1865 514777
or e-mail: info@infideas.com

Where it's at...